TAO OF DAVIS

CHERYL WOOD

TAO OF DAVIS

CHERYL WOOD

This book is set in Verdigris MVB Pro Text. Designed by Mark van Bronkhorst, the typeface strives to replicate the metal letterforms of 16th-century punchcutters such as Robert Granjon, Hendrik van den Keere, and Pierre Haultin while meeting the demands of contemporary designers. Titles are set in Optima.

ISBN 979-8-7855-3012-6

Production and design by:
Reidhead & Company Publishers
www.reidheadpublishers.com
Bishop, California

*This book is dedicated to the individuals
with intellectual, developmental, emotional, or physical differences
that render life more challenging, and to those committed to coming up
alongside as caretakers, as advocates, as teachers, and as social workers,
in the labyrinth of special needs.*

TABLE OF CONTENTS

MAP   IX
FOREWORD   XI
PREFACE   XIII

PROLOGUE   3

I	DETOURS AHEAD	9
2	BIRTH WRECK	13
3	THE BLISS AND BLESSING OF IGNORANCE	17
4	DANCING WITH DENIAL	21
5	LEARNING TO BEND	31
6	POTHOLES	35
7	DOING DAVIS	41
8	THE DIAGNOSIS	47
9	BRAIN DRAIN	51
10	BOTH OF ME	59
11	SWEET CHAOS	65
12	RUNNING WITH THE HERD	71
13	NEW HORIZONS	79
14	THE SAD SOUND OF SILENCE	83
15	REMEMBERING OUR ROOTS OF LOVE	87
16	DING	93
17	FROZEN NANNY	101
18	SHUNT FUNK	107
19	A LIFE FULL OF FLIES	113
20	MOM TROT	123
21	DO ALL, BE ALL	127
22	DIALOGUE WITH THE DIVINE	133
23	PLANS?	147
24	AGING UP AND THROTTLING BACK	151
25	CRISIS, WHAT CRISIS?	159

26	THE SHARING OF TALES	165
27	TAM OR HURKEY	169
28	PLAN Z	179
29	MAYBE THIS WILL WORK	187
30	LOSING A MENTOR	193
31	CHERYL STRAYED	201
	EPILOGUE	207
	ACKNOWLEDGEMENTS	213
	APPENDIX	215
	THE AUTHOR	221

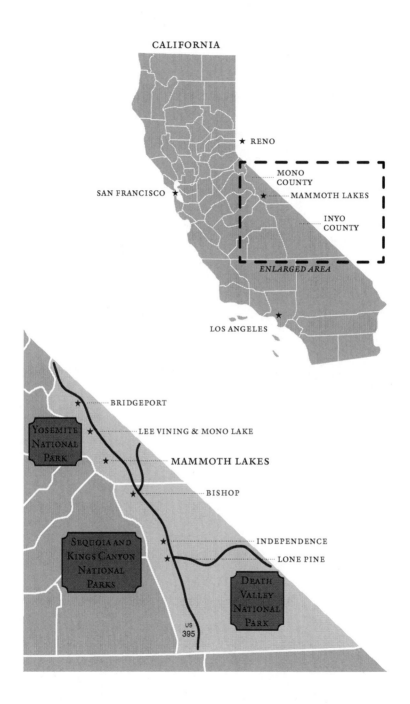

CALIFORNIA

★ RENO

MONO
COUNTY
SAN FRANCISCO ★   ★ MAMMOTH LAKES

INYO
COUNTY

ENLARGED AREA

★
LOS ANGELES

★ BRIDGEPORT

YOSEMITE
NATIONAL   ★ LEE VINING & MONO LAKE
PARK

★ **MAMMOTH LAKES**

★ BISHOP

SEQUOIA AND
KINGS CANYON   ★ INDEPENDENCE
NATIONAL   ★ LONE PINE
PARKS
DEATH
VALLEY
NATIONAL
PARK

US
395

FOREWORD

By Katy Phelan, PhD

There are many definitions of "rare". Some involve being infrequent, scarce, or unusual in occurrence. Others describe being remarkable or extraordinarily good. In *Tao of Davis*, Cheryl Wood relates a parent's perspective on raising a child with a "rare" genetic disorder known as Phelan-McDermid Syndrome (PMS).

In November 2021, the Phelan-McDermid Syndrome Foundation reported that fewer than 3,000 families worldwide have registered as having PMS. This genetic condition is truly infrequent, scarce, and unusual in occurrence.

As with many families I have had the pleasure of meeting, Cheryl and her husband Rick have experienced the highs and lows of dealing with a rare disease. They have dealt with the unknown and unusual with grace and humor—some swearing, some wine, some bargaining, and always with friends and other rare families to offer support.

Cheryl and Rick embraced the PMS family support group and evolved from participants to instructors and advocates. They shared information to help other families consider their child's current education and therapy plans and to reflect on their child's future. They have been and continue to be valuable resources for other families affected by PMS. They embody the remarkable and extraordinarily good aspects of being rare.

Tao of Davis is the gift of one family's insight and experience in daily life with a rare disease. I trust that others might see themselves, family members, or friends in these pages. The second gift that the frustration, acceptance, and humor in this book offers is hope. Please read and enjoy!

PREFACE

"For there is always light if only we're brave enough
to see it, if only we're brave enough to be it."

Amanda Gorman

Raising a child with special needs and a rare chromosome deletion
was not a goal my husband and I set, but rather a circumstance we
found ourselves in. I am conflicted in my surrender and belief that
this cherub carved a fine journey for us both as his parents because
of his peculiar rare disease. There is a reality of painful moments
and parts of our family that will never be whole because we had the
challenge of keeping Davis alive and the joy of giving his day meaning when we could.

What makes a journey meaningful?

The conflicts overcome? The sweet spots in between each challenge? Or simply the process, who I was as I began in earnest to
shape a family to the best of my abilities, and where I learned to shift
my expectations and to forgive myself when I stumbled? To be better
when I could. I will admit that I lacked patience, I fumed. I moved
a bit too fast and furious, and yet, I circled in each time, back to my
soul space. Back to a place of peace where I recognized me, I appreciated the whole of me, and I dissected what I felt did not work or
fit in to that place of peace, called the 'Still Point' by poet TS Elliot:

At the still point of the turning world. Neither flesh nor fleshless;
Neither from nor towards; at the still point, there the dance is,
But neither arrest nor movement. And do not call it fixity,
Where past and future are gathered. Neither movement from nor towards,
Neither ascent nor decline. Except for the point, the still point...

Is it because of my phase in life that I can look back and ahead and not see past or future? All is in the present. Unfolding as if in today, in this moment. The Still Point is my secret garden, my place in a whirling landscape of what has been, what is, and what may yet unfold.

As I write this my son growls, demands, calls to me in the only way he can to fix his world. Change the cartoon. I do, and we cuddle, he smiles, and I return to sum up why it is I need to tell our tale.

We, each of us, can return to our still point when the winds outside knock us down. We can get up. We can become bruised, scarred, and fatigued. And because we have, we know we will again, and that the only rainbows in our life are in that whirling world beyond the quiet. I continue to step back into the storms because of what is on the other side. There is always a sun ready to warm us, always a sea ready to still our frenetic minds. Always a friend to cherish our heart.

This story is about that chase for the other side after each storm.

THE TAO OF DAVIS

Prologue

PERFECTLY MAUI'D

"Look closely at the present you are constructing.
It should look like the future you are dreaming."

Alice Waters

1993

I stared out toward the volcanic shoals which framed Kapalua Bay
on the island of Maui. The night before, Rick had explained to me
that Kapalua meant "arms embracing the sea"—and then he had
proposed. I had accepted. That morning, we returned to set up
chairs by the water and enjoy the vista. Beyond the edge of the *arms*,
the waves broke boldly enough to occasionally lure out a surfer. I
tested the word *fiancé* in my mind, and I smiled contentedly as I
daydreamed about building a family and future together. I lifted my
hand so that the diamond in my new ring sparkled against the blue
of the ocean. In the distance, I saw the islands of Lanai and Molokai
above the horizon. The soft foam of shore break lapped up over my
toes as I wiggled them in the wet sand. Yes, I thought. *I like this: the
fiancé, the future, the family.*

On the north part of the sand, close to the beach shack with paddleboard and canoe rentals, I watched a family preparing to play.
Two children close to the ages of Rick's son Ryan and my daughter
Lynnell scrambled to claim a canoe. I guessed they were between
four and nine years of age. Not quite old enough to paddle alone.

A parent climbed in beside the older boy as another parent adjusted the young girl's life vest.

This could be us, I thought. Smiling. Eager to push off into the sea. Ready to splash one another with our paddles. Blending two families into one. Yes, I nodded as the group headed out into the peaceful cove. We will be a family smiling back at the world as we make our way into an amazing future.

Do you hear me, universe? I silently asked as I looked up. *This is what I want!*

Just then a strange cacophony of sounds, a mix of squawks and resounding staccato shrieks, caught my attention. Others on the beach turned their gazes toward the disturbance as well. A loud man acting like a child lurched past me on the sand toward the sea. His body appeared to be unstable, tilting, moving quickly without the apparent strength or capacity to move well at all. His arms flapped like wings as the strange sounds he made broke the quiet peace on the beach. What I heard seemed unintelligible. He stopped near the water and began to hop from one foot to the other, still off balance.

Two more people, a grey-haired elderly couple, moved past me to catch the odd man. They did not seem to notice that those of us on the beach were an unwilling audience. We preferred the sounds of the distant waves to the nonsensical noise of the man in the sea. The odd man stopped moving and squawking when the older couple joined him. The chaos settled for a moment. A second woman, younger than the couple and seeming to defer to their guidance, joined them carrying a set of fins, a snorkel, and a mask. I stared, transfixed by the spectacle.

The older woman placed the snorkel and mask on the strange man's head. She adjusted it tenderly to fit across his face. Her words seemed to capture his attention as he stared at her. The grey-haired man led the man-child, as I defined him in my mind, further out into the water with gentle surf slapping at their calves. Slowly and steadily, they moved into deeper water until they were up to their waists in the tranquil bay.

They placed a fin on one of the odd man's feet, and he toppled over sideways, unable to catch himself. His mask was askew on his face. It took minutes for the three caretakers to get the odd man to his feet so that they could place the next fin on the other foot. Their patience exhausted me. Eventually, the awkward man floated face down, guided across the shallow reef by the older man. As the two women stepped back toward the sand, I was thinking, "What an embarrassing set of circumstances for the young man and those caught up in his orbit."

The older woman looked in my direction. I was gawking, and, in that split second of eye contact before I turned away, I knew that she had read my thoughts as I judged their situation as sad and their life experience as less than my own because of an apparent disability.

In my blind chase toward Happily Ever After, I did not see that the universe had a better plan.

1994 Christmas Letter

So many momentous events have occurred for Cheryl and me in the past two years.

First, Cheryl and I met in February '93 when she moved her business to a suite in the office building in which my offices were located. Love at first sight? Yeah, it still happens...

My law practice was and is growing nicely, notwithstanding that the economy here in this vacation playground has been difficult during the past few years. I continue to emphasize business and tax matters, and I seem to have found a niche professionally.

Cheryl's business, Phoenix Professionals, has grown remarkably during the past eighteen months. She currently has placed computer program analysts throughout the United States in temporary assignments. Fortunately, she can conduct business from our location without having to rely on the local tourist trade. In April, we combined and expanded our offices to a new location and can work together every day.

In September, Cheryl and I traveled to Maui and became engaged. In October, we purchased and moved into our new home in a neighborhood reminiscent of the 'old days'—kids crawling out of every house. Schools are adjacent to the neighborhood, and we feel the kind of safety and security that seems to be present only in small towns like ours these days.

In February '94 Cheryl, myself, Ryan (mine), and Lynnell (hers) "sneaked off" to Maui again and were married on the beach in Wailea in the rain. We had a wonderful week there, and although family and friends were necessarily excluded, we had a memorable ceremony in which the kids were our witnesses.

Now, for the kids. Ryan, who is nine and a half, has shown serious interest in my favorite sport, skiing. He is on the mountain race team and was fortunate enough to win the "Kittredge Cup" in '93. Lynnell, who just turned five, left 'babyhood' behind, is growing into an active child and 'challenges' us all. She has also followed Ryan by taking piano lessons. You can imagine what our house sounds like! Last but not least, we are expecting our first child together next August. We are looking forward with great joy to 'doing it over again.'

Happy Holidays from the Woods

1

DETOURS AHEAD

"Interrupting our destructive habits and
awakening our heart is the work of a lifetime."

Pema Chödrön

1994

In Hawaii, rain is considered to be a blessing, even a good omen,
if it happens on the day of your wedding, which for us it did. We
stood with the minister under an alcove near the beach in Maui as
the water dripped from the eaves above with Ryan and Lynnell as
our witnesses. Ryan stared intently as the minister spoke of our
union as a couple and as a family. Lynnell tried to pluck a plumeria
from Ryan's lei. The boys wore the blue traditional formal Hawaiian
short-sleeved shirt. Lynnell wore a mumu. That morning I found a
traditional Hawaiian white on white with a subtle floral pattern and
put it on just before the ceremony.

"Cutting it a little close," Rick had said when I walked in holding a
dress to wear for the wedding. We had been looking for a few days
for what I knew would appear. I trusted the Universe. So far all had
gone well in our courtship and elopement. I knew a dress would
'pop up,' and it did. After the ceremony, the rain stopped and Rick
and I walked toward the beach to have a few wedding photos taken.
I looked up and silently sent my gratitude back and up. *Thank you
for this.*

In the easy early months that followed, Ryan called me mom, and Lynnell called Rick dad. The initial awkwardness of dinners and outings together dissipated as we learned more about one another. No tomatoes, potatoes, ground beef or beans for Ryan. No early dinners for Rick. Lynnell, she scampered close beside me like a pup unsure of where her new place in our home would be. I tried to let her feel she had my complete attention, as we had been a team of two once, much like Rick and Ryan. Then I became pregnant. We were ecstatic, and my heart felt full as we awaited our new child.

Early in the pregnancy something began to gnaw at my mind and body. The pregnancy felt different; something was off. My pregnancy with Lynnell had been physically easy, but emotionally challenging. I had been single, unwed, and very much alone. *Why was this time harder?* I wondered.

The feeling was strong enough that we decided to have an amniocentesis, a screening for developmental abnormalities in the fetus. We looked at the test as a simple precaution. The clinic was in Sacramento, on the other side of the towering Sierra Nevada mountain range. In good weather, it was a five-hour drive across high mountain passes and through steep-sided river canyons. The long drive afforded us time to ponder the question that dominated our thoughts: What would we do if something was actually wrong?

Despite our fears, the limited test told us the child was a boy and indicated that no apparent genetic issues were present. I never questioned that my child could less than a beautiful, perfect little boy who we would call Davis. In blissful ignorance, we never answered the question that continued to lurk in our minds.

The return trip home from Sacramento quickly transformed into more of an ordeal than the procedure itself. The strongest, wettest storm of the winter slammed into the Sierra. Snow clogged the mountain passes while at the lower elevations rain inundated hillsides and flooded into rivers.

We made it east over the snowy passes near Lake Tahoe and then turned south onto the road that would take us home—U.S. 395.

The scenic highway 395 follows the Sierra Nevada's eastern escarpment, north to south. Rain cascaded down the mountainsides. The windshield wipers beat furiously back and forth. The deluge was too much for the weak soils of the surrounding hills, and soon the earth was beyond saturation. Just before we reached the narrow canyon carved by the Walker River, a mudslide rushed across the road and slammed into a car ahead of us. No one was hurt, but the road was impassable.

We diverted course and made it home fourteen hours later. Five feet of fresh snow blocked our way from the car to the front door. Rick helped me slide over the powdery snow and into the warmth and comfort of our home. Past the worst, we made light of how strange the adventure had been and looked forward to the birth of our child.

———

My contractions began in month five.

At the time, having a baby in the mountain town of Mammoth Lakes was logistically challenging. We lived in "a perch atop the world," as Rick liked to say. Far, far away and 8,000 feet high, to be exact. Los Angeles lay five hours to the south, less if Rick drove, and Reno was a three-hour drive north. The closest hospital that delivered babies was almost an hour away and down the hill in Bishop—a slightly larger town sitting at 4,150 feet at the foot of the Sierra. My obstetricians, a team of two, were in Bishop. With contractions in play, Rick and I raced down the hill toward the hospital where my obstetrician's office had directed us.

Why had we chosen to live in such a remote area? Didn't we feel isolated amidst the mountains and high desert, asked friends and family from anywhere else. Did we miss the malls and movie theaters? No. Did we miss the people who lived elsewhere, in the big metropolis of Southern California? Of course.

But we also had found a slice of paradise. Independently, the two of us had fallen in love with the expanses of granite, forests, and meadows tucked up against the sage and pinion pines. I had lived in Mammoth in my early twenties for five years. I left to pursue an MBA in Orange County. Rick moved to town two years before I returned. Our future together as a family of five felt promising, but we knew it was too early to be having contractions as we dashed down to Bishop and the hospital.

Rick, frenetic, pulled into a parking space and ran into the lobby while I was left struggling to unbuckle my seatbelt. The painful, hard contractions slowed me down. Delicately, I maneuvered myself off the seat, onto the hot asphalt, and toward the front door, my hands braced against parked cars as handrails. I was almost there when Rick reappeared with a look of chagrin. The check-in desk wanted a patient.

Once I finally made it into the hospital, I was admitted for monitoring. The contractions mysteriously stopped after a few hours. We left the hospital with our nerves unsettled and a warning to take it easy. I spent the remainder of the pregnancy lying down.

Something was amiss, yet I refused to heed the signals, and nothing could have prepared me for what would soon turn our family life upside down.

2

BIRTH WRECK

Americans: This is the Captain of a US Navy ship. Please divert your course 15 degrees to the North to avoid a collision.

Canadians: Recommend you divert YOUR course 15 degrees to the South to avoid a collision.

Americans: THIS IS THE AIRCRAFT CARRIER USS ENTERPRISE, THE LARGEST SHIP IN THE UNITED STATES ATLANTIC FLEET. WE ARE ACCOMPANIED BY THREE DESTROYERS, THREE CRUISERS, AND NUMEROUS SUPPORT VESSELS. I DEMAND THAT YOU CHANGE YOUR COURSE OR COUNTER-MEASURES WILL BE UNDERTAKEN TO ENSURE THE SAFETY OF THIS SHIP.

Canadians: This is a lighthouse. Your call.

A fictional tale on the Internet

1995

Our doctor gave us bad news on the day Davis was to enter the world.

"The baby is breech."

I didn't react immediately, and the doctor repeated herself, thinking I was slow to understand, "Cheryl, the baby is breech."

I got her message, her pronouncement of a problem. I just didn't want to hear it.

An ultrasound confirmed the doctor's suspicions.

A nurse administered a shot of terbutaline, a drug commonly used to relax the uterus so that a baby in the breech position can be turned. Rick and I decided to walk the hospital hallways as we waited for the medication to kick in. The hall began to spin, my face cooled, and my head tingled. Rick guided me back to the room where I collapsed. My arms spasmed as I slid to the floor. I resisted the weight upon me with every muscle, but I could not stop whatever was happening to me.

Later, I would learn that I had experienced several side effects to the drug, including an increased heart rate and dizziness.

My body continued to melt. A nurse placed a blood pressure cuff on my arm. Her voice tremored with alarm as she called out the numbers, "Sixty over thirty."

The nurse's voice faded. My stomach did a free fall, carrying me along as I rapidly lost the sensation of life. I could not connect to any part of me. My arms flapped to the side, my legs weakened as if melting, I wanted to vomit, and I desperately wished I could just close my eyes and make the craziness stop. My physical control swiftly eroded, leaving little time to feel fear or defiance. My only desire was to make everything stop, even if that meant to stop all the way, to leave, to die—but I wasn't even aware that leaving could mean dying. I just needed it to end. The taste of bile seeped into my mouth, and a foul sweat covered my skin. I tried not to throw up. I continued to slip into a space that felt dangerous and unstoppable.

Suddenly, I wasn't dropping, but floating up. My nausea and fear were gone. I saw the woman with the big pregnant belly below. She was me.

My mind shifted back into my body and an awareness that my baby was in trouble as the nurses tried to get me to the bed and place a strap around my belly to monitor our infant's heartbeat.

"The baby!" I screamed. We needed to help the baby.

The nurses positioned me on all four legs as though I were a dog. I spiraled downward into fear and hopelessness in the face of the terrible circumstances.

The doctor returned to a rapidly deteriorating patient. Plans changed in an instant. Rather than turn our baby into position for a natural birth, my situation now required a Cesarean. Someone led Rick off to change into surgical garb so he could be present for the delivery. Another team wheeled me into surgery. They moved fast while I crawled from the gurney to the operating table. I stared into a blinding white light as an anesthesiologist appeared and placed a plastic breathing mask over my face.

I felt the life draining out of me again as monitors sounded more alarms in response to my dropping vitals. I saw a chaotic swirl of nurses and doctors rushing around me. The sounds of these alarms would follow me through the decades, and I lived in fear of them. Their banshee wails would turn my stomach and freeze my blood any time I heard them from that day on.

Suddenly the alarms stopped, and Rick was led into the room for our son's birth.

The sheet covering my stomach jostled as unseen persons jerked my body back and forth, but I felt no pain. Then, the delivering surgeon lifted a silent child into the arms of a waiting pediatrician. The room was dead quiet.

Our baby made no sound.

I wanted to cry. My eyes darted to the corner of the room where the pediatrician pumped on my son's tiny chest. The beeps from the monitor grew as our son's heartbeat regained its strength. The room inhaled the deepest breath I ever heard.

My doctor pulled on my open wound and stitched me up, but a deeper gash remained. One she could not fix. One I would deny for years to come: the flawed birth had stolen from me an ability to feel safe and protected in this world.

I disappeared into a deep sleep once Davis was taken to the nursery. The out-of-body experience had left my mind muddled and foggy. I wanted to close my eyes and wake to a better day.

3

THE BLISS AND BLESSING OF IGNORANCE

"Thanks to the miracle of modern medicine, we expected and believed that pregnancy would be uneventful and birthing would be a beautiful, extraordinary event. We would count the number of fingers and toes, and if they added up to ten plus ten, we assumed that our child would be perfect. The possibility that something could go wrong was a distant, unformed thought that did not apply to us."

Rick Wood

1995

The pediatrician stopped by the following morning. His brow bore the weight of bad news.

I looked away, unwilling and unable to face more flaws in what I wanted as a good birth experience.

The doctor told me that Davis had a heart murmur and that this was not good. I also learned that his head circumference was the largest of any baby ever delivered in the Bishop hospital. Though this too was a cause for concern, the doctors were affectionately referring to Davis as Charlie Brown. I tried to see the levity in the name, but I could not. The only good news was that Davis had not been deprived of oxygen at birth, but all the other signs of possible problems overshadowed this news. By evening, we learned that Davis would need a life-flight to Fresno because his situation required a better-equipped hospital to address the heart murmur and enlarged head. More tests were needed. Rick and I stood together as the hospital staff wheeled our newborn son down the hallway—his weak cry barely audible above the scurry of feet pushing a plastic capsule on wheels. I saw only a little plastic container that resembled a casket as the life-flight team transported him away across the Sierra to Fresno Children's Hospital. I buried my face in Rick's shoulder, and my desperate negotiations with God began.

My father, a former chaplain, would have called this prayer:

Hey up there,
our little one is in trouble.
Please help us.
Please stay close.

Three excruciating days passed before I was released from the hospital in Bishop. Rick and I immediately traveled to Fresno to be with Davis, who was in the Pediatric Intensive Care Unit. It was a sweet relief to hold my baby in my arms, yet Davis was lethargic and less responsive than a healthy baby. By the end of the week, we received some much-needed good news: the two issues that had prompted the life-flight had been resolved successfully. Davis's heart murmur had been due to a poorly operating valve between the chambers in his heart. The valve had not closed properly after birth, but medication fixed that. His oversized head—called *hydrocephalus*—had been caused by an excess fluid buildup within cavities deep inside the brain. Fortunately, this resolved on its own.

Spending time in a children's hospital produced two distinct revelations. First, not all babies were equal. Some lived, some did not. Some were broken, some were fine, though all were premium. Second, even a casual stroll through various wards offered scenes of hope and despair, and through it all, an undying belief that once we got out of there, everything would be okay.

Once Davis was back home and the birth wreck was behind us, we surrendered to the bliss of ignorance. Davis remained "floppy"—foretelling issues with his brain and body to the trained eye—but since we were not experts in developmental disabilities, we simply settled in adoring our newest little family member.

I determinedly reclaimed my vision for our family, confident that the crisis was over and that the landscape ahead could and would return to all that was once so wonderfully familiar.

4

DANCING WITH DENIAL

"Denial helps us to pace our feelings of grief. There
is a grace in denial. It is nature's way of letting in
only as much as we can handle."

Elisabeth Kubler-Ross

1996

Who knew first?

Rick. Rick knew that everything was not okay with Davis long
before I could conceive of any imperfection in my sweet baby.

Rick's shoulders drooped more quickly than mine. His sleep
became fitful. His need to be away arrived faster. Rick became
president of Little League and coached Ryan's team in the sum-
mers. His hours in the office became longer as he became our sole
income provider. Earlier I had been proud to have made the down
payment on our home because I had earned enough through the IT
staffing business I had started. I had run my nationwide business
from a distance in Mammoth until Davis arrived. Then my attention turned to his care. He was slower, less responsive, and less alert
than other babies. I absorbed what I could about the lack of development apparent in our new child. Still, I also purposefully looked
the other way to avoid the unfamiliar landscape I would later know
of as disability.

Our boy's life-flight after his birth had brought him to the attention of education and health experts in various departments in

our county offices. Programs existed to monitor and assist children with developmental delays or health issues. In my mind, *delay* meant an option to catch up. I kept this hope front and center as Davis, Rick and I attended our first meeting when he was just three months of age.

The meetings began with a health assessment by Dr. Feldman, who reminded me of Santa Claus, beard and all. Plus, the holidays were coming, and Christmas was on my mind.

Doctor Feldman, aka Santa, began to check my son's arms and legs—referred to by others as floppy. He smiled, he complimented me on my choice of outfit for our son that day, matching socks and all. He stayed behind to write up his notes before joining us with the next group. This team would change over the years but initially included educators, health care support providers, physical therapists for Davis, and family therapists for all of us.

Rick placed his notepad on the conference table. I placed Davis on my lap. This too would be an oddity that would continue far into the future. Even at age sixteen, Davis would still be sitting on my knee in family photos. Patterns started early.

Rick wanted and needed to know more than I did. His pen flew across the yellow page. I peeked over to pick up a few words like "palsy," "floppy" (again), and "developmental delay."

"What is cerebral palsy?" he asked in one meeting when Davis was about six months old.

Darn him, I thought.

"This is cerebral palsy," Santa replied, referring to our son.

The team had handed him a book on the topic of cerebral palsy that day. Rick read it, cover to cover. When he finished, I set the book on a shelf to collect dust.

"Fifty percent of these children are retarded!" he threw at me one evening.

"Well, fifty percent aren't!" I yelled back. At least not mine.

We only knew the word "retarded" as an abstract term because neither of us had ever personally known a person with cognitive challenges. But individuals with developmental challenges had only one name from my childhood memories: retarded. We were new to understanding what words were offensive or appropriate for our child.

Retarded, offensive.

Disabled, appropriate.

———

As we celebrated Davis's first birthday, I watched my father while everyone else watched Davis combat crawl toward his new toys.

Rick once described my dad as one of God's good people. A humble man who wanted to know another person's story. A man who listened, who never shamed us if we messed up, and who had a calm presence that settled a room and invited everyone around him to be better than they ever imagined. He believed in his children and then in his grandchildren.

That night he watched Davis crawl to the toys, and my father's face bore a combination of sadness and pride that said it all. He and my mother had backgrounds that included disability: he as a retired school psychologist and Air Force chaplain, and my mom as a special education teacher. They were both licensed psychologists, and they knew.

"I think he does an excellent commando move," Rick's sister Cindy said. Bless them for not telling us more. I nodded and refused to see or acknowledge that Davis could barely crawl. He wiggled his fragile, weak body toward the colorfully wrapped presents arranged all around him in a circle on the floor. Most toddlers are good at crawling and use their arms and knees to do so by their first birthday. Lynnell took her first steps at nine months. I understood milestones met and milestones missed. Davis could only crawl forward on his belly feebly toward the closest first birthday gift.

I scooped him up and carried him to the kitchen to set him in his highchair. I belted him in because he was not yet able to hold himself in an upright seated position for more than a few seconds. Another milestone missed, one usually accomplished by six months. With a large piece of cake on his tray before him, friends and family sang Happy Birthday and Rick blew out one lonely candle that almost wasn't. A birth wreck, a life-flight, and a hard start to life.

I admit I threw the first piece of birthday cake that night. Davis smiled when my husband retaliated and nailed me back. Lynnell and Ryan had more time to aim, and Davis picked up what ended up on his tray and put it in his mouth. We continued the play as our guests laughed. I deserved this fun. We all did. Part of me knew something was not working well for Davis. I needed to laugh, to pretend, to deny.

I cannot remember who won, only that the kitchen lost, and my heart felt lighter. The topic of cerebral palsy needed to wait to take up space in my brain. We, the Woods, wanted and needed to feel like a typical family for the moment.

As our second Christmas with Davis approached, life settled, sort of. I learned to church-it-up a bit when others asked how we were doing.

"We're fine," I responded, knowing that in our case *fine* meant *fragile*, like china.

"Davis spices up our day," I explained before describing his antics: he drank from the dog's water bowl, he tried to drink from the toilet (yes, he was still rug bound), and he peeled off his soiled diaper for guests as a gift. Time passed and Davis made little progress on those darned childhood milestones. I stepped into my days frustrated and unavailable to anyone but my son. I felt responsible for his limitations and for my inability to help him catch up. I often wondered, *can he catch up?* I diligently tended to his many needs by taking him to physical therapy, occupational therapy, and family therapy—all while doing lots of smiling to the world so no one frowned back.

SEASON'S
GREETINGS

"We got this!" became our family motto.

But what a mess. Davis's bowels were loose, his butt was too small, his diapers slipped off with ease, and he shimmied too often on his bare bottom across the carpet, leaving a brown trail behind him. We resorted to duct taping his diapers on, and this worked. Sometimes. I stopped pretending to be perky when cleaning up poop.

At two years old, Davis could pull himself up but still could not walk. Falls became a way of life, and we became regulars in the emergency room for stitches. These were all big deals to us, the idea of stitches, of ear tubes, of a sacral dimple that needed an MRI because of a potential spina bifida issue. We were new to medical emergencies, to what was a serious issue, and what was not. A few months after Davis's second birthday, our first major emergency room visit and hospital stay occurred. Ryan dashed into our bedroom after we had helped everyone get settled in for the night.

"Davis can't breathe!" he said, panic in every syllable. "He fell out of bed, he's gasping."

We ran downstairs, I swooped Davis up, and Rick drove us to the Mammoth Hospital emergency room just a few minutes from our home. In these early years, when we ran to the ER, Lynnell was with us, pasted against a wall. Quiet. Watchful. She did not want to be away from me, her mother, but I had to focus on tending to her brother in crisis. What she absorbed through these chaotic moments, how she interpreted her childhood, would haunt me in the years to come.

Under the fluorescent lights, my son's frightened eyes locked onto mine. I sang, which always settled Davis a bit. A nurse tried to take him out of my arms, but I motioned her away and sat on the gurney with our child in my lap as the doctors began their examination. A nurse leaned in with an oxygen mask. Davis hated masks. While I sang, I took his mask off, dismantled the facepiece, and placed the nozzle close to his nose. The song was one of his favorites, about an old man who played knick-knack on his thumb:

> *This old man, he plays two*
> *With a knick-knack paddywhack*

I wanted to scream, but instead, I sang. The singing settled my breath and then my mind; it always did. Davis gasped, his chest rapidly expanding and releasing what little air he managed to take in. The veins in his neck stood out as his muscles contracted with the struggle. The monitor showed a rapid heartbeat.

"What happens if his heart stops?" I asked the young doctor as he injected a steroid into Davis to open up his croup-constricted airway.

"Oh, don't worry about that," he responded with a smile. "We can jumpstart him, get it going again."

Like a car, I imagined, with this guy as the mechanic. I snarled at his remark. We had already lost several young children that season in our small community. My sorrowful song continued.

> *This old man, he plays two,*
> *two small children turning blue,*
> *with a knick-knack paddywhack...*
> *Neither one was mine.*

I sighed with this new fear of our small child turning blue.

———

The crisis ended, and Davis and I returned home from three nights in the hospital. We retreated to our living room couch, Davis tethered to oxygen and me tethered to him. After I put him to bed, Lynnell crawled into my arms, eager to reclaim her own space next to me.

"Mommy," she asked, "when is Kapalua going to have puppies?"

Our dog? Puppies? I had forgotten to update her in all the commotion of late.

"She can't, honey," I said gently. "She's been fixed."

"Fixed?"

"Yes, it means she cannot have babies."

Lynnell wailed, "That's not fixed. That's broken."

Broken, I thought, *like so much of late.*

I snuggled with her, and she eventually fell asleep. Lynnell, Davis, and I spent a lot of time on that couch recuperating. Meanwhile, the dormant volcano under Mammoth Lakes stirred. Thousands of small earthquakes rocked our small community as magma shifted within the earth's crust that year.

During our vacations in Hawaii, I had learned a traditional story told there—Pele burped from her volcano to remind us that we are but guests on this good earth. Geologically, the ground shook to adjust to the tension within. For the Wood family, we had to settle into the new landscape of medical fragility.

"I love your smile Davis," I shared as we snuggled and the earth trembled. Davis loved to hear his name and connected to my gaze immediately. *I love to smile!* I thought his eyes replied. His small hand reached for mine; his heart was already there within me. My gratitude that we could be home again, cuddling, prevailed against the anxious fear of losing him.

During our time on the couch, I became aware of the deep panic within me that I hadn't recognized until the trauma of Davis's birth. Davis's hand, Lynnell's hug, Rick's kiss could always bring me back to a place of optimism and belief that we were all okay. Ryan was not a hugger; when I tried, he would drop his arms to the side to endure my embrace. Still, his all-boy energy and kindness grounded me. I straddled two worlds with my emotions: on one side was the fear of loss, while the other foot was rooted in a trust that the world Rick and I were creating for our family would be good for all of us. The pinch of the pain from my fears made the softness of the snuggles even sweeter because they made me believe we could be okay again.

Davis shimmied off the couch, done with the touch time. He did his four-limbed scramble, which was still not quite as coordinated as the full crawl that his therapists and teachers were trying to help him learn. He aimed for a toy truck, which he turned over so that he could spin the wheels.

"Ya. Ya ya," he shared. Translated, *I am happy.*

"Me too, buddy. You make me happy, too," I said.

Happy Holidays from the Woods

1997 Greetings from the Wood Family. Here's what's happening in our World.

First, we're all doing fine. Even though we live and work in God's country, we feel like every other family of five: busy. Not enough time to experience it all, so we do the best we can.

It has been another year of challenges for Davis, now two-and-a-half. He recently spent a few days in the ICU at Mammoth Hospital for a respiratory problem. We're still not sure where his place in the world will be, but we continue to hope that the extraordinary care and therapy he receives will result in a normal, happy life for him. Fortunately, his medical issues have been resolved by three minor surgeries this past summer. He is truly a gift who has forever changed our lives. With three kids, Cheryl and I have moved from man-to-man to zone defense! Davis has permitted us to see the world a little differently than before and to recognize that each of us has, in our own way, something to give to others.

Lynnell, now eight, our free spirit, continues to excel in school, and is skiing on one of the mountain teams for the first time. Perhaps she will follow in the footsteps of Ryan, now twelve-and-a-half, who is the top-seeded racer at Mammoth for his age group, and who is considered one of the top three racers in the far western United States.

Speaking of skiing, that seems to be all we do (well, Ryan and Lynnell play baseball, soccer, piano, drums, etc. in their spare time—you know how it works). Snow skiing started in September and will continue through April. We will then pull the boat out of storage and waterski/ wakeboard until September. It seems that both of those activities provide something for everyone in the family. Last summer we took several camping excursions to lakes in and near the area, and we spent eight days on a memorable houseboat trip.

As for us, Cheryl has stayed in shape by running this year, even in the snow. I continue to practice law, participate in local politics, and run the little league each Spring.

This has been a year of settling for us.

Despite what you have seen and heard over the past several months, Mammoth Mountain is not going to erupt. There is significant movement of magma (short for volcanic lava) two miles from here, and we have had thousands of earthquakes over the past six months, but fewer than one hundred have been stronger than 3.0. When we get one (we feel several nearly every day lately), the kids don't even look up from what they are doing. Do we sound complacent?

Come on up to the mountains and enjoy the clean air, pristine wilderness, and skiing. Anyone who receives this letter is welcome to stay (provided, of course, that it is not for too long!).

We hope that this next year brings happiness and success to all of you.

Happy holidays.
The Woods
Rick, Cheryl, Ryan, Lynnell & Davis

5

LEARNING TO BEND

"Patience is not simply the ability to wait—it's how
we behave while we're waiting."

Joyce Meyer

1997

My father wrote all of our family Christmas letters from the first
year of their marriage and well into his late eighties. His natural
preacher style of story-telling captured the attention of our relatives
and friends as his Air Force career took us away from them to Spain
and Okinawa when he was stationed out of the country.

When Rick wrote our first family letter, I felt initiated back into
the traditions I had grown up with. I played hostess to the holiday
celebrations, the family reunions, the friends and neighbors gathering for a meal.

When he wrote the second holiday message, after skipping a few
years, I felt a dark shadow creeping toward us from the horizon as
we acknowledged the challenges our newest family member faced.

The last few meetings with the county team in charge of Davis's
development, or lack thereof, became part of that approaching
storm. The specialists in education and health who tracked our son
since his difficult birth continued to drop bombs on our hopes for
progress each time they assessed him.

During the last meeting with our team just before Christmas, one
of the specialists handed me an essay entitled "Welcome to Holland."

It was supposed to make me feel better about this new opportunity to travel to a place I never packed for. The author described the challenge of disability as a missed trip to Italy. The essay ended up in a drawer. *Not yet,* I thought, *and not sure when.* Meanwhile, a thick file labeled "Davis Wood" lay open on the conference table. Rick was beside me as Davis fidgeted on my lap.

"Look, I just need to know one thing," I smiled as I spoke. *Had it really been two years since we first met this team?* So many therapies, special programs, and still so little progress made by Davis.

The faces before me remained serious, unflinching in their professional rapport. *No return smiles? Oh well.*

"Do you think Davis is retarded?" I asked. I wanted them to assure me that Davis would be okay in the long run.

Silence.

I hated this type of silence, the pause preceding disaster.

"Yes," someone said, almost in apology. I could not tell who had spoken because my eyes were cast down toward Davis.

"Severely," she added.

Retarded?

This word echoed incessantly in my head—*retarded, retarded, retarded.* Memories of kids taunting other kids on the playground with that word—*retarded*—and the stigma of it flashed through my mind.

Davis's occupational therapist, Sharon, entered the room, unaware of the current conversation. I looked up at her with tears streaming down my face. "Is it true?" I asked. "Davis is retarded?"

"Oh honey," she responded, bending toward me, hugging me, hiding me from the rest with her embrace. "Oh honey."

I knew this. Rick knew this. We already knew this. But I didn't want to know this, not out loud, not yet.

I was on Prozac not long after the meeting. My doctor had recognized my melancholy long before I did and, after a second suggestion, I gave it a try. Perhaps Prozac was on me, shielding me from what tugged me down. Our expectations for Davis were worlds apart from our experience thus far. Everything was different. *Why was Davis different? Why would he never catch up with his peers? Different.* That word repeated in my head, too.

Why did I struggle against this concept? That word had defined my life choices and so many of my experiences before I became a parent.

My parents made it look so easy, to raise a family, to provide experiences unique to each of us. To love.

What am I missing? I asked no one in particular the next morning as I took my run in the woods.

Snow had not yet buried the paths and silenced the birds. I asked aloud because I knew the forest had ears, but lacked the capacity to throw back a verbal answer. A chipmunk scurried off, perhaps I had yelled too loud. A pine cone *thrwumped* to the ground. Then an owl hooted.

Dad.

The symbol that most reminded me of my father was the owl. The wise watchful owl with the capacity to see all sides as its neck twirled right and left with ease. The owl reminded me not just of a mentor, but of two key pieces of advice I didn't listen to as a teenager, and again ignored well into my twenties: Trust the process, and don't lead with your chin.

This was a moment to trust the process. To stop comparing my idealized childhood to the chaos our own children faced with the medical issues of our youngest child creeping into our lives like a storm still brewing, not quite ready to rain on our hopes and dreams. Not yet.

My mind settled and heard a new tune as the wind rustled the aspen leaves about. Radio Psyche, that connection between the deep unconscious level that otherwise pounced up on me in my dreams. Lyrics. These came from Beth Neilsen Chapman and Don Schlitz. I heard them first when sung by Tanya Tucker. The words held promise of redemption for an otherwise rebellious decade before I had Lynnell as a single parent and then met Rick. When I used to 'lead with my chin.'

> *Like a tree out in the backyard*
> *That never has been broken by the wind*
> *Our love will last forever*
> *If we're strong enough to bend*

It was time for me to bend.

6

POTHOLES

"We must embrace pain and burn it as fuel for
our journey."

Kenji Miyazawa

1998

"It's just not fair!" I unleashed.

Damn the pothole and my stupid ankle.

I had slipped and fallen, and now I lay in the cold, wet snow. I
was lightly dressed for the short walk from our home to Davis's preschool early intervention classroom at the rear of the elementary
school, but I didn't have time for self-pity: a thirty-pound, two-and-
a-half-year-old Davis sat heavily on my lap, and his portable oxygen
tank pressed painfully into my back from the fall. My ankle badly
hurt too.

*Ugh. Do I crawl and slide over the snowbank with Davis and his medical
gear?* The backdoor to our home looked as if it could be on the other
side of the Sierra Nevada mountain range.

This sucks.

I wanted to cry. I was angry, frustrated, and tired. The school's
empty playground, visible from my crater in the snow, mocked my
loneliness. The pity party turned on, and I cursed the gods because I
wanted more from my tribe—I wanted them to do what only I could.
The truth was that Davis preferred me. We all knew it. If he saw me

pass by, he would cry until I scooped him up in my arms. Anytime I needed to be alone in another room, Ryan and Lynell had to throw a sheet over me to sneak past Davis. They called it a game, but I felt entrapped by his desire to be in my arms and my desire—my responsibility—to make life better for Davis. Carving a piece of joy out of a short hike or a run made me feel worse when I returned because he rarely did well when I was not beside him, making his world better. I woke up with dreams of trying to scoop him away from a giant wave or pulling him to safety from a cliff.

I knew I was only one of many caregivers tending to a fragile child in this world. So why did I feel unique and as if I deserved a break—though not in my ankle that was caught and twisted in the snowbank? I didn't deserve anything, but the unfairness of it all was intolerable at times. This was not what I had hoped for or expected as a parent.

Davis fidgeted on my lap, anxious to be moving and out of the snow. I could hear his thoughts, *Hey, let's move!* He liked to be in motion. I opened his backpack and searched for a distraction. I pulled out a toy truck, and he spun the wheels and smiled. *Wheee!* he exclaimed without words. *That was fun!*

Sorry, sweetie, mommy is on hold until I can figure this one out, I thought as I worked to get us out of the snow.

"Ya, ya ya," Davis said with enthusiasm—his version of "this is great!"—as he continued to spin the truck's wheels.

I admitted to myself that I had been distracted and missed my footing today. Okay, truthfully, I had been absent since I chomped off a bigger piece of truth than I could handle about Davis and his latest potential diagnosis.

This is a new pose. I thought. *New extension. New strength. Get comfortable. Stay awhile.*

My thirty-plus years of yoga practice began after college with Manju, the son of a famous international yogi named Pattobois Jois. While I was finishing my MBA, I lived in my parents' VW camper and attended his studio one or two times a day. Manju pushed me and about fifteen others toward and beyond intense discomfort, to the other side—and there was another side.

Manju was short in stature, broad-shouldered, and had an accent that dropped the *r* in my first name for a *d*.

"Chedyl," he would say. "Pay attention."

I am trying to, I wanted to say to my imaginary Manju that day in the snow. But the current pose challenged me: the pose called Davis.

In my mind, I heard him reply as he used to when he adjusted one of my poses: *take slow deep breaths, get comfortable, move beyond the pain and hold the pose.*

Remembering his Indian dialect soothed my mind. I felt the space between my shoulders and ears give a bit as Davis turned the wheel on his truck and my butt froze in the snow.

Breathe.

Session upon session, the routines well in place, breath became my magic carpet, lifting me from the monkey chatter of my brain and easing the tension caused by fighting the pose, the place, the movement.

"No pain, no gain," he would declare this chant in the clipped consonants of another continent. I started each day in his small studio with his other devotees. Manju navigated his way in and around our contorted bodies. He would pull an arm through lotus-legs or push on our backs when we declared we could go no farther into a pose or an asana. The twang of a sitar and the pungent scent of bodies hard at work created the façade of an Indian ashram. Beside me, a man would exhale, much like a snake, and ease further into a pose while sweat dropped to the mat beneath his nose. Beyond him, an older woman with the agility of a cat flowed through her workout. We were the regulars.

During this yoga period in my twenties, I parked my campervan near an all-night gas station to sleep. In the morning, the sound of waves and the smell of the ocean aroused my senses the way the spurt of a coffee maker and its brewed aroma would later initiate my days. I balanced this phase of drawstring gauze pants with my pursuit of an MBA up the coast at the University of California Irvine. Chants and tank tops juxtaposed against graphs and business suits.

Sitting in my crater in the snow, I wore neither as I reflected on my early days of devoted yoga and Davis became restless. I missed those days. I missed the quiet of Manju's wisdom.

"Like a Barbie doll!" Manju would say as he swung my leg up behind my head. "Chedyl, pay attention."

In his studio, the essence of my study was a process of releasing. Parts of my body surrendered as I pushed through a pose. I would become aware of yet another set of muscles or ligaments, layer upon layer, over time. One challenge gave way to another, and through it all, I breathed.

If he were in the snow with Davis and me, Manju would probably remind me, "No pain, no gain!" and encourage me to get my butt and my little boy home. I would tease him back as I used to when something registered as a bit more than uncomfortable—"Oh good! I must be gaining!" That always did make him smile.

I had to peel back new layers of awareness—muscles of the mind— to unveil Davis's differences and disabilities, his gifts and abilities. It was Davis's differences that would make him the gatekeeper of our family. Early on, Rick and I noticed that people who felt uncomfortable with our boy's inaudible communication or who were unable to greet Davis as they would any other child, well, we didn't want them in our life. He beckoned good souls forward and thwarted those with callous hearts unable to attend to anyone less than perfect.

The Tao of Davis demanded deeper awareness and attention. It invited me to release my expectations for him and fed my desire to be the hero who would enrich his life, my life, and our family's experience.

I wanted a Disney ending, yet I now found myself in this pose, which demanded that I remain ever-present, not looking back and not hoping to rearrange our futures. I had to be steady. My unheroic role would be to tend to his feeding and toileting needs, to decide on a life path, and, perhaps, to help him to contribute to the world around him.

Davis's differences, particularly in the beginning, made me uncomfortable and very protective. I observed the reactions of others and, though I was not sure he knew when others stared at him, I felt the need to defend my son. One time at school, two young students who passed by us referred to my boy as "loco." In my broken Spanish, I explained to the children that Davis was different. "No está loco. Es especial."

With Davis's peculiar noises and lack of interaction with others, I was not embarrassed, not disillusioned, just off-balance in my effort to protect him. It took years to gain my footing, my positioning. Years. I had once considered my yoga years to be an escapist period, but the experiences in that studio proved to lay a solid groundwork for my life with Davis.

My time in that dark, dank former dance studio was as invaluable as my hours in the lecture halls which finally led to a Master's degree in Business Administration. I acknowledged both paths with two frames on my office wall: in one hung my degree, in the other a picture of a series of yoga poses that I called "The Labyrinth of Yoga." My Master's degree represented an achievement of the ego, the mind. "The Labyrinth of Yoga" represented an opening of the heart and the soul.

Pay attention, I heard Manju say again. *No pain, no gain.*

I yearned to be back home. A sprained ankle? *Shoot, we've got this.* I took that first painful step and thought, *Manju, I must really be gaining.* Ouch.

Breathe.

Davis smiled as I prepared to stand up and haul us both up and over the snow and back to our house. My shuffle was painfully slow, weighted by Davis and his gear. I worked my way home to call for help. Someone else would have to take Davis to his preschool early intervention program. I had a date with an ice pack.

7

DOING DAVIS

"Even as we grieved, we grew."

Poet Amanda Gorman

1998

As my ankle healed, I chose to re-engage with the circumstances life had dealt us. I could not change our reality—that we were the parents of a child challenged by physical and cognitive limitations. I found the book on cerebral palsy that Rick had read, and which I had cast aside. I blew off the dust and read it cover to cover. I began to reach out and ask more questions of other parents I met with children like my own. I learned to accept my fears about the strange new place I referred to as the labyrinth of disability and special needs. Eventually, I felt ready to read the unwelcome essay that one of Davis's specialists had given me: "Welcome to Holland," by Emily Perl Kingsley. I had since received a second copy from my sister-in-law Janice, which was a sign that this essay wanted me to read it. Kingsley, a former writer for Sesame Street, had a son who was diagnosed with Down syndrome. Her words were timeless:

> When you're going to have a baby, it's like planning a fabulous vacation trip—to Italy. You buy a bunch of guidebooks and make your wonderful plans. The Coliseum... The gondolas in Venice. You may learn some handy phrases in Italian. It's all very exciting.
>
> After months of eager anticipation, the day finally arrives. You pack

your bags and off you go. Several hours later, the plane lands. The stewardess comes in and says, "Welcome to Holland…"

I happened to like the idea of dikes and windmills, Don Quixote style, but here Holland represented disability or difference. The parents, of course, were disappointed. Ms. Kingsley encouraged them to settle in and enjoy the detour. Get new guidebooks, learn the language. In her essay, we, the parents of children born different, would eventually learn to appreciate this other place. But the loss of the dream—the perfect trip to Italy—and the pain from that loss was real, she said.

Ya think? I thought while reading it.

But that part about settling in to enjoy the detour? *Poppycock.* I still had a bit of fight left in me about what I felt entitled to, and it included Italy, not Holland. In truth, I wobbled between accepting the Tao of Davis and whining during challenging moments. I accepted some parts of the journey and struggled against others depending on my mood or the space in my life to gracefully embrace my circumstance. For me, this was the dichotomy of dealing with disability.

I did not deny the detour, but it took time and patience to submit to embracing the tulips. My younger self would have said "Game on!" to any new challenge. However, as I adjusted to living with disability, I preferred to tiptoe toward each cliff, not wanting to see what was below or blocking my path. Rather than tackling the challenge head-on, I was coming to terms with the fact that our life would not be as picture-perfect as I had once hoped it would be. "Doing Davis" was our new quest, chosen or not. The problem was that I did not want to define myself as the parent of a child with disabilities because, maybe, if I did not, I could turn this trip around and get us back to familiar ground that did not include the destiny of disability for Davis.

Our lives and routines morphed around Davis. Medical appointments with specialists in the bigger cities found their way onto a calendar that once held only activities for the older kids' sports and school schedules. Rick took on the task of shuttling Lynnell and Ryan to soccer while I was Doing Davis.

After 'crisis' there was such sweetness to the ordinary. The rush of our children on a school morning as they headed out the door. The walk with a friend into the forest around us. The cat basking in the afternoon sun in our kitchen sink beneath a west-facing window— west to the mountain which drew both Rick and I to this place.

Still, so often, when the older kids asked me for help with something, my response was, "I can't right now, I am Doing Davis." *I'll be there as soon as I can,* was implied. The message I later regretted: I prioritized Davis over his siblings.

Rick and I stumbled into the world of disability like two travelers denying we had turned a wrong corner and might be lost. We knew where we wanted to go, and after each wrong turn, we found a few markers to redirect us on our path. Our destination, which we knew to be true in our hearts, was to have a child who could be independent, cognizant of his care, and capable of living on his own. We did not want Davis to be passed on as an inheritance into the hands of his siblings one day. While Rick and I were in Holland for the long haul, Lynnell and Ryan didn't need to be.

Rick deftly took the lead in filling out paperwork and enrolling us in government support programs, including California's unique Self-Determination initiative. When Davis was still very young, we qualified to receive sugared-up formula to help our skinny baby boy grow. When it became apparent Davis would not potty train any time soon, diapers were delivered.

The diapers turned out to be a disaster as did the sugared up formula. The thin oversized diapers slipped off quickly and required duct tape to hold them in place because our son had a very tiny butt.

He would slide out and leave a mess in his wake until we could get the duct tape to stick more securely. We learned to double up his diapers when we were having guests or the children's friends over because the trail Davis left was, well, gross.

We also had to learn to adjust to Davis's many other special needs: he walked slow and ate even slower. Feeding required vigilance because Davis was a stuffer. Like a chipmunk, he popped whatever was in front of him into both cheeks. At school, this once resulted in an aid applying the Heimlich maneuver on him. As for the sugar formula, Davis developed a mouthful of cavities that required repair under anesthesia in a hospital three hours from home.

From the time Davis was a young boy, we attended countless therapies and meetings. We had to be in so many places to provide physical hands-on learning or to meet with Davis's specialists and discuss what they were doing and why. Rick took notes at the meetings, and I glanced at a word here and there on his notepad. At the end of these meetings, the team would hand us a list of new places to go and people to see. Soon it was time for a geneticist. Did I want to know what was truly different about Davis? Not really, not yet. So far, all of my efforts had had little impact on the ever-increasing gap between where most children would be and where our son was.

Nonetheless, we decided we were ready to know why Davis was different. We made the trip to the geneticist a family affair and hauled the entire tribe down to Bakersfield, four hours away.

The first pronouncement out of the geneticist's mouth was that Davis could remain bald the rest of his life. She said this before doing any blood work, any in-depth interviewing, or any eye contact with me, his mother. I hated how she pulled back a veil on his future so abruptly before any diagnoses had been offered up. In truth, we had not yet done the full genetic tests because I was not ready to know some things. Rick had left this up to me because we were both scared, but he knew I might not be able to absorb a full diagnosis yet.

I felt that the geneticist was a poor fit, and I wanted to find a new one. As was typical when I could not absorb more bad news, I looked the other way. In this case, I gazed at my son. He would have hair, I decided. Like everything else about Davis, his hair was just taking its time.

We drove the four hours back to Mammoth from Bakersfield and, as I carried Davis back into the house, I heard him say *B-r-r-r-r*, his version of *It's cold!*

Note to self—get a hat for Davis when he is out in winter.

On a summer day in the Sierra, I was in a line at McDonald's when I noticed a woman in the other line, holding her child in her arms like I was—both too big to be carried and obviously not typical. I changed to her line, stood behind her, and said, "They just get bigger, don't they?"

She turned, and we shared tired smiles. Our bodies both swayed with fatigue. Her boy smiled. I smiled back. His eyes seemed to say *Mommy's worried a lot.*

He's like me, my boy seemed to reply as he reached toward her son.

I introduced myself and Davis. She did the same for her and her son Seth. Once our orders were in, we sat together and fed our sons. Her family was off hiking in nearby Red's Meadows. This was her activity, to sit and eat with her child who could not hike. For a few precious moments, we shared stories about our lives alongside disability. Oddly enough, we were both smiling, perhaps because we understood each other and could validate each other's experiences simply by listening. I learned that Seth was regressing, both in health and mental capacity. I learned that hope has many faces, one of which was called "acceptance." She still had Seth, and with this came hope. Over the years, I would learn to seek out like-minded mothers in that strange land of disability because together we could share our stories, and with this came healing, soul to soul connection, and a sense of empowerment as we navigated the faint twists and turns of our unexpected detour to Holland.

8

THE DIAGNOSIS

"Fear is a natural reaction to moving closer to the truth."

Pema Chödrön

1999

I was alone with Davis, five nervous medical students, and a kind, well-spoken geneticist named Dr. Graham on the day my son was officially diagnosed in the spring of 1999.

Davis tugged at my hair and reached for the pen in the doctor's coat pocket. The students leaned against the walls of the tiny examination room, and one or two smiled as my son succeeded in pulling a pen from the doctor's pocket. Bored with the pens, Davis poked at my nose, then tried to work his hand down into the front of his diaper. I repositioned his hand and continued to listen to words I was not yet able to comprehend: chromosomes, deletions, genetic tests available that were not routinely administered when we did the original amniocentesis. That part scared me. If I had known back then when I was pregnant about Davis's issues, what would I have done? What would we have done? I loved this child so much it hurt. I constantly feared for his welfare. My soul ached when I pondered life without this simple sweet soul to remind me and those around him that we all can be uncarved by life, unaffected by jealousy, anger, fear, or desire. Perhaps he was more whole than the rest of us.

And I was frightened for his future.

I turned my attention to a diagram in a report the doctor wanted me to read. The picture reminded me of worms lined up in pairs. The worms were chromosomes. We each had twenty-three pairs of these. Chromosome analysis meant that the smallest part of these worms could be analyzed for a disturbance. In Davis's case, the problem was that he was missing a piece of DNA on his twenty-second chromosome. Just a snippet, really.

The doctor informed me that thirty-three other individuals were known to have the same deletion, called 22q13.3, on the twenty-second chromosome. Years later, the families of individuals with a deletion on 22q13.3 would officially name this condition Phelan-McDermid Syndrome (PMS) in honor of the researchers who first identified the anomaly. That day, I learned that Davis happened to be the thirty-fourth person in the world to be diagnosed with a deletion on 22q13.3. *The thirty-fourth in the world?!* This felt like an unfair game of *Tag, you're it!*

The doctor handed me a report about seven other patients with Davis's new diagnosis, later known as PMS. I skimmed the paragraphs, searching for clues about what my boy could be like, and I found that all seven participants were under the age of five.

Davis fussed on my lap, and all eyes were on me. The silence in the room made me uncomfortable. *Why were the children in this report all under the age of five?* I thought.

"What happens to them after the age of five?" I whispered.

No one knew the answer.

Did they live past five?

At that moment, I was struck with the searing anguish that any parent feels when faced with the terrifying possibility of losing their child. I simply could not bear to lose my boy— I felt this to the very core of my being— and I could not let the fear of losing him taint the hope that made Doing Davis possible. I needed to hold onto the idea that Davis's sweet, simple soul would continue to bestow its gifts upon me, my family, and our community. *Please*, I asked of all that was benevolent in the universe, *let him live beyond the age of five.*

The doctor handed me a card for Dr. Katy Phelan, PhD, one of the two specialists noted for discovering PMS. She had been gathering the families of children afflicted with PMS into a support group. Our doctor suggested that I call Dr. Phelan to join her group and learn more about my son's condition.

Nope. I would not call. Some information was best left on the shelf, I felt. I was not ready to accept this diagnosis or its lousy prognosis.

Some students stared at us, while others shifted about with palpable discomfort. So much remained unknown, and so much was unspoken. *Were they scared for me?* I wondered. *For Davis? For our future?*

I resented the concreteness of the diagnosis that would follow him, follow us, forever. *Cry later, in the car, while he sleeps,* I thought, but my sadness was too overpowering. Sorrow arrived in that room full of strangers, and I wept.

The day before the genetic diagnosis from Dr. Graham, Rick and I had met with a neurosurgeon, Dr. Levy, to discuss another issue: the results of a recent MRI. Both specialists were in Los Angeles, which was helpful—even if driving our whole family five hours south to the city wasn't exactly convenient. Rick and I drove separately, as he had court appearances and our other children to tend to. We joked that killing three birds with one stone on this trip was efficient.

Davis had undergone surgery the prior year to fix poor eye muscle control, or "wandering eye," but afterward, the doctors had noticed that he had a pale left retina. The MRI was ordered to investigate the reason behind this observation. In Dr. Levy's office, we gazed at the MRI film, which showed two large cysts in Davis's brain. The doctor explained that one cyst was the size of a peach, behind the left eye. The other, on the brain stem, was the size of a golf ball. Both needed to be removed. As I slowly and painfully processed this news, Rick and the neurosurgeon discussed brain surgery. I stared at the black blobs on my son's brain and thought, *Thar be the Dragons*, that unchartered area on ancient maps where sailors feared to go.

Rick and the doctor compared their calendars and arranged a time for surgery. I had no calendar anymore. I Did Davis. My schedule revolved around his ever-changing health needs. Rick had headed back to Mammoth Lakes after the appointment with Dr. Levy to tend to Ryan and Lynnell while I had ventured on alone to meet Dr. Graham for the genetic diagnosis the following day.

———

In the weeks leading up to Davis's brain surgery, a piece of me shifted, as it needed to. A warrior stepped forward, and a weeper stepped back. My heart was on lockdown until we returned to Los Angeles for the cyst removal. I could not and would not explore the PMS diagnosis or the opportunity to reach out to Dr. Phelan, who had set up a family support group, until we passed over this first awful threshold that I feared would take Davis from us.

Rick and I did not share any details of Davis's conditions with our older children. We knew so little about what the future might hold for Davis—except that he might not live past the age of five, thanks to the article that I had stuffed in my nightstand drawer—so we sheltered the kids from these unknowns. Ryan and Lynnell merely knew they had to stay elsewhere—Ryan with his friend's family and Lynnell with my parents—while we took Davis to Los Angeles for a procedure. We did not think that this situation would nurture the widening chasm between Ryan and Lynnell as siblings to each other and to Davis. We supposed that we would be gone for just two nights and that when we returned, we would play board games and make summer plans around the dining table as a family. Rick did return in two days. I did not.

9

BRAIN DRAIN

"When we least expect it, life sets us a challenge to
test our courage and willingness to change."

Paulo Coelho

1999

Rick and I brought Davis down to Los Angeles for surgery together.
Rick approached the event as our next hurdle. I held back, fearing
for the worst: that it might also be our last with Davis. The chromosome deletion article haunted me, and the idea of brain surgery
shattered my hope for normalcy.

The goal was for the surgical team to remove the two arachnoid cysts in Davis's brain. When the procedure went longer than
expected, Rick and I began to panic. We paced the hospital halls,
we called friends and family, but we did not openly discuss our
deepest fears with each other. Finally, the surgeons came out to
talk to us. Blood was smeared across their aprons, on the sleeves
of their gowns, on their caps. "What did you say he has?" one of the
surgeons asked.

We told them the little we knew of the deletion, and they went
back into surgery.

Hours later, we heard from the surgeons again. They informed
us that they needed to place an exterior shunt on his head to manage the excess fluid. After this, they said, we would be allowed to
see Davis.

When we finally stood beside our boy again, gauze covered his head and a tube came out the top. Tubes were also in his arms, and another in his mouth. I immediately realized that our son was in trouble. He did not wake up after the surgery, so we were told to come back in the morning. I was heartbroken that I could not remain in the hospital beside him for the night.

Rick and I left the hospital empty-handed, heavy-hearted, and at a loss for how to express our sorrows and concerns to one another. We preferred to focus on the positive—we liked to think of ourselves as the *rah-rah* team, who could get through problems big and small together.

We stayed at my brother's home that night. I stepped out into their backyard and Rick followed me. I cried. He held me. We stood like this as the wave of fear swept over us and through us like a slow freefall into an abyss we may not survive.

That night, around midnight, we called the nurse's station to check on Davis. We were told that he had stirred a bit, that his shunt had stopped draining (as if this was good, but how would we know?), and that they had administered morphine to settle him. We slept, hoping disaster had been averted. We returned to the pediatric intensive care unit (PICU) the next morning to discover that our child and his bed were missing.

We panicked.

"Where is my son?" I asked. One nurse stepped away to find an answer to where my son was, while another nurse asked me to leave.

"I want my son," I said again. "Where is Davis?"

"Can you wait outside please, you're disturbing the other patients," the nurse I immediately dubbed "Godzilla" growled. Her patients were in cribs and appeared to be not even a year old. She was big, but I felt bigger. I was a mama bear searching for her child.

"No. I am not moving. Tell me where he is."

"I hate the way they treat us here," Rick muttered. He turned to leave.

"No," I said again. "Tell us where our child is…please."

The first nurse returned and sent Godzilla away. She motioned Rick forward, her voice soft, her compassion apparent. I was scared. "He is having an MRI," she explained this and looked away from our gaze, "But I cannot say more than that." She did not meet our eyes. "I'm sorry. The doctor is with him and will come out to talk with you shortly. Please, let's go outside, to the waiting area."

While we were in the waiting room, some family members arrived: first my father, then my brother Paul and his wife, Janice. Rick and I said little because we knew so little. Eventually, our doctors showed up and explained what had happened: the night nurse had not received proper training for monitoring a brain procedure with an exterior shunt. The shunt was meant to drain the excess fluid in Davis's head so that it would not build up and create pressure in his brain. The night nurse had made a mistake when the tube malfunctioned and stopped draining, and now Davis had yet to regain consciousness.

The doctors told us that Davis needed still more surgery to fix his condition. We signed more forms, prepared for more surgery, and approved a plan to transfer Davis to the nearby Los Angeles Children's Hospital, where the better trained staff could deal with his *situation*.

We were now in a situation.

I was numb.

Hours later, after yet another surgery, we returned to the PICU to wait with our still unconscious Davis for the ambulance transport team. Davis was swaddled, from head to toe, in bandages and tubes. His eyes remained shut, his body so small, so still.

The department head of the PICU approached. We were silent as he spoke. He wanted us to consider the possibility of long-term care if Davis did not come out of his coma.

Coma?

Together, without words, both Rick and I decided that this doctor must be wrong about long-term care. Doctors had been wrong before. As if to confirm this, Davis moved his arms and briefly fluttered one of his eyelids. I stepped toward the metal crib a few feet away. Rick followed. We gazed down at our child that they would not let us touch or hold.

I saw it again from between the layers of gauze—a flicker, his lids half open—and my heart leaped. "Davis," I whispered because I knew he heard me. "Davis, I see you. Oh, honey, I see you." Rick was beside me, and he too saw the tiny response. The PICU doctor approached along with the nurses nearby. I didn't care if they saw what I did. I knew he was with us. Healing. Alive.

The ambulance transport team arrived and prepared Davis for his trip across town to Children's Hospital. I rode in the ambulance. Rick followed in our car. Once there, Davis was wheeled into his own room. A nurse dressed him in new colorful pajamas and invited me to hold him.

"Really? I can hold him?"

"Of course you can. That's part of his healing," the nurse insisted. She even smiled. "You sit over there, and we'll adjust the bag to the same height as the top of his head where the tube is located. See, it drains into the bag."

Rick snapped a photo of us—me with a big smile, holding my son, who was not yet four years old. *Did he have another year?* I wondered. And at that moment, I surrendered. Whatever the pace of healing required, I would be there. I would listen. I would not let fear steal this precious, finite time we had. And once I made this choice, I resolved not to know the survivability rate for the children in his genetic group, with a deletion on the twenty-second chromosome. With my new plan determined, I settled in.

"He will be dizzy if the fluids are not level," his nurse said as she guided me through how to hold and help him. Davis's eyes were open as she said this, and I learned what to do. For the next four weeks, my job was to hold him and assure him that I was with him as he drifted in and out of his morphine stupor and mended from the surgery.

The next few days involved waiting to see what Davis's body could do. Would the excess brain fluid drain properly or not?

The brain fluid drained into a clear plastic sack. At first, the sack beside his head appeared to fill with fluid that resembled a dark burgundy. During the next week, the color in the sack slowly lightened to rosé as the excess blood in his head cleared. Then it became a chardonnay. The nurses used these vintages as marks of healing and progress. *Would I ever look at a glass of wine the same way*, I wondered?

During that first week, in the morning, on my cot, the sound of voices near Davis often awakened me. Medical students and a doctor discussed my son's condition as I leaned forward with the thin blanket pulled closer to my chest. During one of these discussions, I learned that Davis had suffered a brain infection and would require a ventricular shunt to be placed in his skull with a tube that would drain the excess fluid from the brain into his belly. The next surgery would take place once the infection ended. We again hunkered down for a long period of healing.

Davis often watched me from beneath his morphine-induced trance as the respiratory therapist held a nozzle near his mouth for his lung medication, which was administered through vapor. He would reach out his hand toward mine, and I would stroke the inside of his little palm. With this, he peacefully drifted back to sleep.

I constantly nodded off to sleep, only to be awakened by a cry of pain. Then I would ring for the nurse, who would swiftly appear with another shot of morphine for Davis. She would check his vital signs, check his fluid bags, and take Davis out of his crib to arrange him on my lap. We would sit together for hours until the next shift of nurses came to help move him back to his bed. This was our routine throughout his healing

After four long weeks of convalescing and the placement of a ventriculoperitoneal shunt, Davis was deemed ready to go home.

As the nurses removed Davis's IV to get us ready to leave, I saw why my poor boy, who could not speak, had been so difficult the last few days. The site of the IV had a burn mark from the morphine.

No one had checked the insertion point. They asked to keep him an extra day. I refused. We needed to go back to Mammoth Lakes, to our familiar beds, with our loving family all around us.

———

On my first night home in Mammoth Lakes, I found myself pacing around the living room at two o'clock in the morning while my family slept. My sleep pattern was still stuck on the four-hour rhythm of the nurse's vital statistics rounds from our long hospital stay. I settled into a chair, turned on a light, and reached for the study that the geneticist had handed me months ago about the seven children with Davis's chromosome deletion, PMS—the paper that had caused me to wonder: *What happens after age five?*

Rick woke up around six that day. He found me on the sofa crying. In the safety of his embrace, I unveiled a new host of fears about Davis's mortality.

"I think you should call Katy Phelan. She started a family support group." As he spoke, Rick guided me to the kitchen for a cup of coffee.

"I will," I lied. My goal was survival, and I was not sure that I could handle more disturbing news about my son's diagnosis.

———

Being home did not last long. After barely a week, Davis appeared to have vertigo. He sat crooked with his head tilted, and he threw up his food. The doctors determined that the shunt was malfunctioning and the surgery to make it drain properly needed to be redone. We needed to return to the hospital in Los Angeles.

The boy I placed in the back seat of our car was a whisper of his former self. As I settled him into his seatbelt, I felt the bristle of his shaved head. I gently stroked the incision sites, one on the side of his head to remove the cysts, one on the back of his head for the shunt, one on the top of his head for the exterior shunt. This top one was still swollen, like a button on a turkey to tell us, "I'm ready. Done!" *Was he? Could the next surgery work?*

Lynnell climbed into the car beside Davis, though she would stay with my parents at my brother's home in southern California. My family stepped up so that I could step out, again, with our youngest family member. For how long I could not know or say.

As I drove back to Los Angeles to deliver my son to the surgeons, I was tuned tight in the key of fear. My nerves felt like fine china in a batting cage, ready for the breaking. I allowed my biggest fear to come forward in my mind: *Could Davis live?*

Then, the cell phone chirped, interrupting my thoughts. I flipped open the receiver and listened.

"Cheryl," Rick's voice crackled through the tiny phone, "I just talked to the doctor on the East Coast. The geneticist. Katy Phelan. None of these kids talk. There is an older one, though, twenty-seven years old. That's good news."

So much for ignorance providing me with some form of bliss. Rick abruptly revealed a reality that was not all that scary after all. I took a deep breath as I processed this information—there was an adult, someone alive past the age of five. Thirty-three children and one adult. With another deep breath, I thought, *I can do this. We can do this.*

"At least we know we have him for a while, I guess," I said.

"Oh, and all of them wear diapers—even the oldest. One has been placed outside the home. The others are still with the families," Rick added.

Suddenly I felt faint, lightheaded, and I quickly said goodbye.

I heard only one thing in the echoes of my mind: *A-a-a-a-r-g-h!*

———

A few hours later, I parked, placed Davis in his stroller, and rolled him into the emergency room as the surgeons had instructed me to do. The doctors thought that the shunt needed to be relocated to perform better, and they whisked him away to fix what was wrong. I was concerned that his genetic condition might not permit the new shunt to perform at all. Thankfully, I was wrong. The surgery was a success, and the doctor allowed Davis to return home after just one night in the hospital.

"Buddy," I said to my sweet son, "we are heading home."

He smiled, a bit hesitant, a bit weak. But still, I knew he understood me. In my mind, I heard him reply: Home.

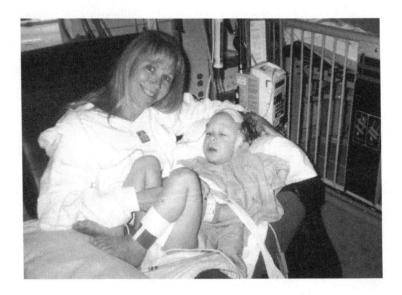

10

BOTH OF ME

"We are meaning-seeking creatures."

Karen Armstrong *The History of Myth*

1999

My identity as a former single parent, a new stepparent, and a brand-new special needs parent always felt driven by the needs of my cherubs. I wanted to be more available and in tune with each child, but I had some shortcomings. I lacked empathy when caught in the vortex of my daughter's emotional outbursts. I took it personally when my stepson exhibited moody silences as he became a teenager. I floundered when coping with Davis's medical and developmental fluctuations and limitations.

I felt less capable in my many roles because constant medical crises tore me away from the family and wore down my patience, sense of self, and consistency. I deeply regretted this. It helped that Rick and I carved out space and time for one another, usually when the children were in school. I called these our "nooners"—moments when we could return to an intimacy we felt was unabashedly ours. I also did a lot of reading and writing to help make sense of my journey beside Davis. I especially read a lot about mythology, including Karen Armstrong's book, "The History of Myth." In it, she wrote a line that I have always carried with me—partly because it sounded like something my father would have said. She wrote, "We humans are meaning-seeking creatures." Her writing inspired me to ponder the purpose—and the possible solution—to the conflict of feeling engaged in my own life while disability tore away at my sense of normalcy. I picked up a pen one day and wrote the following:

"I would like you to return to Earth and work with a family." Archangel Gabriel speaks with a soft voice. The small, sandy-haired cherub beside him nods, then hiccups. Sheepishly, the child looks up, his hand covering his mouth.

"Whoops!" The boy says, without using words, for here the message emerges equally through thought and gaze. Kwan Yin, to the right of the boy, smiles as another burp escapes. Dionysus, playfully tapping his leather cap with two horns, adds his advice.

"Let's do this in the seasons of green. Before the snow."

"Snow. Will there be snow?" the small one asks.

"More than you can imagine," Dionysus responds. "Yes. Plenty of snow. And with this, I can roll out my bountiful spring and nourish our summer."

Kwan Yin strokes the stubborn cowlick on the small boy's head while she quietly puts forward her concerns. "We want to bring their solos and duets together and create the celestial chord called 'family' surrounded by friends. And to do this, we need a miracle."

Gabriel tilts his head. His brown hair brushes against the feather of his wing. He moves away from the group. "Let's call our miracle Davis."

"I will plant the name right away," Asclepius advises.

"You will touch a community, heal many hearts, and weave together souls who could not otherwise be connected. Do you understand?" asks Kwan Yin. She points toward the doctor, Asclepius, and motions him near.

"Will the boy have dreams?" she asks.

"Yes, but he will not have words to describe them," Asclepius explains. "But those around him shall feel the healing of his presence."

Just then, Ganesh, a short, pot-bellied figure with four arms and the head of an elephant, moves forward from a pack of figures behind the boy. "I will be alongside on this journey, to keep the way clear."

The boy smiles and hiccups yet again. He reaches for one of Ganesh's right hands, content to have his pal nearby.

"Well, it is time." This voice belongs to The Supreme, and the other deities honor the command, though they cannot see its source. The sound comes from within, from beyond, and throughout. The message is always clear. They nod in reverence.

"Oh." Gabriel kneels so that he can meet the crystal blue eyes of his ward. "Davis. There is one more thing."

The child remains still, his gaze on the angel before him.

"You will be born different. I mean to say that a piece of you will be missing."

The small boy gulps, suppressing a belch. His gaze drops down toward his satin loincloth. His eyes beg the answer, which part?

Dionysus speaks. "You scare him, Gabriel." The green god removes his helmet with horns and kneels as well. "A part you cannot see will not be with you on this trip. It is a piece of your chromosome. A sliver of a slice, really."

The boy continues to stare at the ground, fixated on one of the red jeweled stones near his big toe. Kwan Yin places her hands on the child's shoulders.

"And no, they will not know how to fix you, or fix your body, I should say."

"And that is part of the healing. Not yours, but theirs," adds Dionysus.

"Well then," Gabriel stands up. He holds out a hand to Dionysus, who also stands, "Are you ready?"

"Hands together, child," Dionysus instructs. "And in you go."

On Earth, my hiccups begin as a child lands in my body and steals my heart.

Though I gained insight and confidence through reading and my written explorations, there was always a child or two to knock me back down to feeling like a clueless parent. It didn't take much: angry words, the wrong lunch fixings, a tardy pick-up from sports practice. I once commented that I could not count on myself to be reliable, and Ryan laughed, not realizing the underlying message was about his brother. My day revolved around the needs of our youngest, so much so that I often broke plans. It was not that I forgot to follow through on something deemed important by the older children; it simply was that I couldn't be in two places at once. This made me feel like I was letting my tribe down and made me feel bad about myself.

Then a friend named Sue showed up to teach me how to remember myself. She helped me see myself not just through my older children's eyes but through the smiles of friendships, of family members who did not judge, and through uplifting connections within our community. Sue had a son named Christopher, who she hoisted about in his car seat. He was seven when I met him. His body reminded me of a three-year-old's form. With eyes that could not find us when we spoke to him, his mind reminded me that some individuals are more cognitively limited than Davis. Despite Christopher's challenges, Sue always seemed to exude positivity, warmth, and humor.

Early in our friendship, Sue gave me a strange gift: a fart machine. She loved to use it when we went shopping together. She would set it under chairs in the shoe department, stand off to the side, and then hit the button when an unsuspecting friend sat down to try on shoes. That darn toy of hers ended up in all kinds of unlikely places. It emitted its obnoxious noises in a bread basket at a banquet and also landed under the seat of a maid of honor for a bride that was not one to roll with fart jokes.

I only used the fart machine in our home, which Ryan and Lynnell thought was funny. Soon they wanted one. Sue was the magic elixir for us to rediscover happiness. Lynnell called her Aunt Sue and quickly took to her unique humor. For years, laughter in our home had not been absent so much as forgotten and edited away because of our focus on Davis. But my tribe and I needed to laugh.

Thanks to Sue's gift and her upbeat personality and support, I began to feel lighter and better capable of steering my own boat, even when it rocked about on rough waters. Slowly I came back into balance. She helped me to forget about *happily ever after* and to instead fight for *happily ever now*.

I remembered to cherish the sweet moments of boating together as a family on nearby Crowley Lake, skiing on Mammoth Mountain with the older children, and camping in a tent with the sounds of the children's deep sleep cradling me like a lullaby. I learned to chuckle when a meal occasionally went awry or when the children mischievously entrapped us in a game they had learned that day in school. These precious moments lightened the stress of days laden with diapers, diarrhea, emergency room runs, and constant reminders of Davis's limitations. As I tried to meet all the needs of all three of our children, I learned to accept small moments of collective joy as a gift. These gifts lay a foundation for hope. I pulled up warm memories of these Keeper Moments when my thoughts needed a lift—like when I would see a typical child of Davis's age happily on their way to school and with a healthy future, and a momentary sadness would come over me. In these moments, I learned to pull forward a memory or thought to serve me better: Davis leapfrogging in the shore break, or Lynnell falling asleep in her snorkel gear, or Ryan walking with our dog Kapalua, who adored him and protected him. These Keepers kept me afloat.

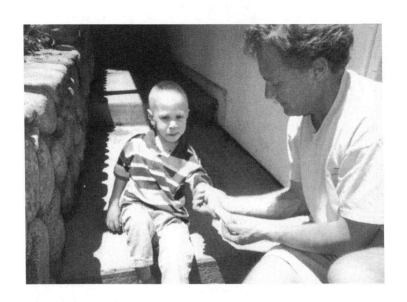

11

SWEET CHAOS

"If you carry joy in your heart, you can heal any moment."

Carlos Santana

2000

What was an easy day like after Davis returned from his surgeries? This morning, like most, had begun with a "bang!" erupting through the baby monitor on the nightstand beside our bed. When Davis woke up, we woke up. Rick reached over toward me for a morning hug once I turned down the volume on the baby monitor. Both of us were grateful for a night of uninterrupted sleep as the household settled back to its pre-crisis routines. I pressed my body into the fold of his left arm and snuggled in.

Next, I shuffled to the kitchen, poured some coffee, and headed to the living room. As fall turned into winter, our Christmas tree dominated the corner of the room. The lights looked great, though the lowest part of the tree was a little bare of ornaments. Gaps occurred where Davis could reach on the tree, on the tables, and in our life. He liked the sound of ornaments smashing. Plates crashing. Still, the top of the tree celebrated the season with angels, wooden toy soldiers, and striped candy canes. Often, at night during the holiday season, Rick and I sat on the couch after the children were in bed and watched the symphony of red, green, blue, and yellow lights on the tree. Sometimes we danced, always to old Springsteen songs.

This morning, I was humming one of the tunes from the night before when I heard another crash from below. I headed down the stairs to the kids' rooms, where I found Davis shaking his baby gate at the far end of the den, which had been divided to give the older children a bit of their own space, too.

"Ya, ya, ya, ya," he smiled as he flapped his arms as if they were a pair of wings, trying to get air.

"Good morning, Davis," I said as I watched him ram his plastic toy lawnmower against the wall. Behind me, I saw Lynnell head for the bathroom, only to discover that Ryan had beaten her to it and locked the door.

The door lock was a testament to the oddity of raising Davis because a key lock was on the outside. Davis learned to lock himself into that bathroom, so I had devised a new entry method. A key hung on a hook which the older children would use to unlock the door. The key went with them into the bathroom to assure privacy. We thought it worked. The children's friends thought it was weird.

I turned my attention to Davis and straightened out his area. I wrapped up the plastic nose piece, called a cannula, and the plastic tubing. I hung these like a lasso on the oxygen machine near his bed. Davis had used extra oxygen at night ever since suffering from croup years earlier. It was then that we discovered that his O_2 levels fell when he slept. Once I unhooked him from his leash-like oxygen tether, he scrambled up into my arms, his favorite perch.

We headed upstairs through the living room to the bathtub in the master bathroom. When I set him down, he scooted toward our room and shut off all of the lights he passed along the way. This was one of his games. Once in the bedroom, he spotted his dad and moved in for a knee tackle. Davis grabbed Rick's hand and pulled him toward the bathtub. Davis loved bath time!

His bath routine included a chase once we had him out of the tub. Again, his game. I followed him with a towel as he headed to the kitchen, my free hand quickly grabbing a diaper and the clothes I had brought up from his room.

Rick was catching up on the national news as our naked child scurried past on his way to the child-sized porta-potty in the bathroom near the kitchen. Then, as so often happened, Davis slipped on his butt. *Oops!* He quickly recovered and resumed circling the kitchen island while I made sounds to make him giggle.

I loved this because our son could only crawl or walk with difficulty before the surgeries for his cysts the summer prior. This morning I felt such gratitude for his newly gained balance and strength. He also liked to find and throw food from the counter with his hand, which he did before I caught him. Our dog gobbled up the muffin from the floor.

Mornings were our time for the first of many potty training sessions throughout the day. I sat on the real toilet, seat down, next to his. Still naked, he mimicked my position. He opened his book, "Once Upon A Potty," and turned page after page. I gently turned the book right side up. He continued to turn the pages and smile. We waited. His hands ventured down below into the plastic bowl to see if anything was happening. Sometimes he could provide a trickle. This morning he let out a bit of a stream. We both clapped. Once diapered and wearing a shirt, he scooted past me. He immediately pulled off the diaper and slid down the stairs on a bare butt.

I was about to retrieve Davis when I heard a crash from the kitchen. A bowl of cereal had simply walked off the edge of the counter because no one was in sight. While I cleaned the mess up on the floor, the doorbell rang.

Seems early, I thought as I went down to open the front door. When I opened the door I found Davis beside our neighbor, who had been out walking her dog. All three were on our front porch: a partially clothed yet undiapered Davis, the neighbor, and her pooch. Apparently, Davis had escaped the house *sans* diaper and then gotten stuck between the front door and the kiddie gate we had installed to keep him from wandering outside. Since his surgery, Davis had become quicker, sturdier, and more explorative. I thanked the neighbor, who appeared a bit skeptical about my remark that Davis had only been outside for a quick moment. I followed Davis over to his room and began to gather up his gear for school. I smiled, eager to believe no more medical crises would weigh us down again, maybe ever.

The other children headed out to their schools—Lynnell out the back door to the elementary school, and Ryan with Rick for a short ride to the middle school. I packed Davis's medical gear and spare diapers into his backpack, then we also left for school together out the back door. I carried him up over the snowbank and into the school parking lot. Then I set him down and we slowly made our way to his classroom at the back of the school. Davis did what I called the "snow boot shuffle," because he looked like he was walking through thigh-high water. He had to push his legs hard to move forward, and the bend in his knee was exaggerated. Still, he was walking.

———

About this time, we adopted the mantra that, "If he can, we can" move forward with a smile. Having come through Davis's medical challenges earlier in the year, Rick and I no longer spoke about his limitations as we once had. We did not ponder his future or ours because of his diagnosis. Instead, we applauded all of the little things that Davis achieved, such as standing balanced, trying to hold a specially designed fork or spoon, stacking items in his therapy sessions, and, something new, his interest in watching the other children play. Davis would go up the ladder to the slide and simply watch others go down. They would move around him, patiently. I watched this from my kitchen window, nervous about where he was but knowing a playground aid stood below, just in case.

Davis's most important characteristic became more pronounced— the beauty of his soul. He embraced any and all. He smiled. He tilted his head when trying to understand something as simple as a child pushing by him in a hurry. Though the kids were sometimes accidentally a bit rough, he always smiled at them. Davis lacked negativity.

He had—what Rick and I celebrated as his gift to the world—a beautiful heart. Through this came a form of surrender in us about our reality, a deeper acceptance of Davis's place in our community and our home. Post-surgery, our family found its footing as Davis lit up our lives. I cared less about the capacity of Davis's mind. As our gatekeeper, he drew kindhearted people into our home. He moved slowly and reminded us not to rush about our day. While he did not speak, he understood moods, felt the sadness in another's demeanor or the intensity of their anger, and reflected this to us simply, uniquely, through his eyes. He made us more aware of our words, moods, and actions. His stillness in moments of hurt or confusion provided all of us a moment to pause and pull our better selves forward.

Walking him toward his classroom, I could see those children who smiled from their hearts and the adults who felt startled by his noises but did not stare or step away. Davis was teaching a whole community how to accept and appreciate a child born different.

"Ya. Ya, ya, ya." My son had words and I understood them when I led him into his classroom. I showed him the sign for *happy* and he attempted to swipe a full arm across his heart up toward his smiling face.

"Good job, buddy," I responded before passing him over to the team of aides, therapists, and teachers that would have him for the next few hours. This was the team that had taught him to crawl through patient and constant manipulation of his arms and feet beneath him; the first of many teams that would lead him forward into adulthood. It would take a whole village to keep our boy healthy and happy.

"Bye Davis, see you soon."

He smiled and wiggled his butt in his earliest rendition of his Happy Dance—his uniquely wordless and joyous way of saying, *I am happy.*

12

RUNNING WITH THE HERD

"The greatness of a community is most accurately measured by the compassionate actions of its members."

Coretta Scott King.

2000

As Davis turned five, I was finally ready to accept and learn about
his diagnosis by engaging with what would become the Phelan-
McDermid Syndrome Foundation (PMSF) support group. Before I
could feel prepared to attend a conference myself, I wanted to talk
with other mothers of children like Davis. I was on phone calls for
a year with a few of the other mothers in an effort to know what life
with PMS was like for other families. I needed to know things on my
terms, before the visual affirmation that would come when gathered
in person at the second-ever biannual PMSF conference in the summer of 2000.

On the phone, the other women and I spoke of our children's similar traits, their developmental delays, and, of course, their unique
cherub qualities. Most of our kids were about the same age. Without
question, all of the mothers I spoke with were devoted to their
challenged cherubs. Yet I still wondered if the other children had a
Happy Dance, or if they were known to skip toward the exit doors
of the emergency room after hours of being prodded with needles in
a way that said *Whee! I'm free!* and brought a smile to everyone's faces.

As the conference approached, I wondered if I truly wanted to know more. I was afraid to learn that Davis's precious smile and his ability simply to be a cute, cuddly soul might disappear as he got older. I also worried that there was more we could have done to help him forward. A big part of me wanted to know more, but I still felt fragile and, at times, in denial of Davis's differences. I feared learning too much at the conference and sinking beneath that weight.

Would the other children have eyes like Davis's? Windows to their soul, their simplicity. The eyes that lead us in, and seemingly define the ones surrounding our simple children who cannot find their own comfort with disability. The eyes that reflect back to us all when one among us is uncomfortable with our children's "difference."

The first leg of our journey to the conference in South Carolina was a flight from Los Angeles to Dallas. I was seated between an older, crotchety, talkative woman with knee problems and Davis—who had people problems. Davis invaded other people's space, so I had tucked him into the seat next to the window. I was aware of others staring at us as we made our way onto the plane and into our seats. Davis made sounds that came out like squawks when he felt excited. He saw Rick and Lynnell seated behind us and, of course, said *Hey, hello!* in a squawk.

"What's the matter with him?" the older woman asked me.

It took me a moment to consider this question. The rudeness and lack of compassion struck me first. However, when I saw my son from her perspective, I saw a boy with one hand on his sippy cup and the other hand, *oops*, in his diaper. He had a big grin. Silently, I removed his hand from the front of his pants and readjusted his shirt.

As the food carts came through, I was careful to shield Davis from grabbing any of the packages presented to him. He had a habit of throwing objects against walls or people. I succeeded in putting away what I could for later distribution, then my seatmate asked again about Davis. I had not answered her the first time, but she was persistent. She was a retired school teacher who wanted to share her knowledge about what I should be doing with my son, who appeared to have behavioral problems.

I faked listening and waited for a break, which came when she offered Davis something from her carry-on bag. He grabbed the wrapped cookie and nailed her in the head with a strong throw. This all happened before I could stop the assault, and then I was apologizing profusely. I stopped Davis as he reached for more from her bag. An awkward silence preceded her response.

"That's okay," she said flatly while she rubbed her forehead. "At least it wasn't the apple."

With that, I decided that I liked her. She may have been cranky and a bit intrusive, but she understood that my guy was not like the others.

———

After two long days of travel, we arrived at the conference for Davis's genetic condition—or rather for us, the families with a child like Davis. At the start of the conference, all of the families convened in the hotel lobby, where I quickly met some of the mothers I had gotten to know by phone. We immediately embraced like family. My own family awkwardly stood back watching what could only be described as mayhem as children escaped the grip of a parent, and many a parent had to chase down their "22q kid." The mothers I had spoken with had used this phrase a few times amongst themselves, and I considered it a type of gallows humor when said by a parent. If anyone else dared used that tag, I would not have appreciated it. This was our walk, our lingo, our children.

As we witnessed many versions of our son dashing across the lobby, lurching awkwardly and not quite in balance, it was apparent that 22q kids had many similar features and habits, like pushing. Davis liked to shove. He found a shoving partner his size, with mannerisms like his own, and the two of them proceeded to topple one another over. One would stand back up, and then the other would shove or be shoved. This continued until we, the parents, intervened.

Some children and some adults with PMS were in wheelchairs, some were running, some were docile, some were not. Some used sign language, some could not communicate. Some parents handled it ever so well in this setting, and some did not. Some had swollen hands or feet, an issue called lymphedema, which Davis also exhibited.

As a toddler, he had developed a swollen right foot from what we thought was a bug bite. I had assumed that this would resolve on its own. At the conference, I later learned that our unique children were predisposed to lymphatic issues, which caused swelling in their arms and legs. Davis's left foot had recently shown signs of slight swelling, so we had bought him extra wide shoes and tried massaging and elevating his foot to ease the pressure. We assumed it must be painful for him, but here again, Davis and the other 22q kids showed a high pain tolerance. They also all appeared to be stuck at eighteen to twenty-four months, or toddlerhood, on the cognitive scale.

In addition to the developmental delays, I quickly spotted similar muscle tone and prominent ears in all of the 22q kids. Davis had adult-sized ears at birth, but he was no exception. Nor was he the only child with a frayed collar. Many of the children chewed their clothes or carried something in their hand to chew on, as Davis often did. Our boy had gnawed the corners of every quilt in our home. When we boated in the summer, he chewed on the waterski ropes.

Sadly, the older 22q patients caused me discomfort. I could mentally embrace the precious toddler stage, but adolescence appeared awkward: they were more estranged from their peers and parents and more isolated in their own world. Bigger would require getting used to, I decided.

At the first cafeteria-style lunch, I wanted to sit with a family who could help us get better acquainted with what may be down the road, years ahead. I spotted a vacancy near an older woman and her son Eric who, at twenty-eight, was the oldest known individual with a 22q13.3 deletion at that time. I led our family over to their table to meet Eric. This was important for me because when I first learned of Davis's condition, I had feared for his life expectancy until I learned of Eric. I wanted to meet him and his parents.

Ryan ate little and stared at Eric, whose mother was feeding him. She was about ten years younger than my mother. Lynnell fussed about in her chair. I listened. They did not get a diagnosis for their son until a few years back. They had simply cared for Eric without much information about his condition for years. They did not know that his 22q deletion caused issues with the lymphatic system and overheating. Instead, she simply went from one surgery to the next and came up with ideas like putting ice packs in fishing vest pockets to cool her boy down in summer along the way. She appeared to be exhausted, without the enthusiasm of some of the younger parents. *Would this be us*, I thought, *eventually?*

Suddenly, Ryan shoved his bowl back and panted, "Gotta go." He took off for our hotel room. I learned later that he vomitted, perhaps overwhelmed, perhaps fatigued from the travel.

It was a lot to ask of siblings, to see so much of Davis's future when they were still in the process of adjusting to so much at home. For the next few days of the conference, Ryan and Lynnell ventured off to the zoo or the mall, mixing little with the other siblings in the group.

Later in the conference, in a room set up for interviews, Davis, Rick, and I sat in front of a video camera and told our story. Actually, I was lying with my back on the floor, balancing Davis on my shin bones as I bounced him up and down in the air. I found myself smiling and explaining to the camera that this was a journey, much like any other, but with a child who required a bit more care and attention. Suddenly, at that moment in front of the camera, the part of me that seeks meaning and purpose—like the *why* of Davis or the timing of an event—found an explanation for us both. Doing Davis was our purpose together, he and I. In the video, the "ah-ha" of this idea showed through.

The capable quest-seeking version of me showed up on that trip. I was edging myself toward acceptance, and it helped to be amongst others on the same path.

Throughout the conference, all of us parents shared our stories, both good ones and tragic ones. We talked of Davis's love of the sea and the shore; how, during our family trips to Hawaii, he rolled about in the shore break, then leapfrogged forward with a small wave and rode in with the white foam. I liked that we talked of the fun stuff alongside the harsh realities we knew to be part of our shared experiences. Rick spoke of Davis's recent hospitalization for his brain surgeries.

At the end of the conference, all of the families posed together for a group picture. The moms sat on the floor while almost hog tying their children to hold them still or pinning them in a chair with their arms. It was bittersweet to finally part ways after the long weekend bonding with the other families and the researchers who were devoted to learning and sharing more about the complexities of this particular deletion with all of us swept up in its wake.

———

We had a long wait without chairs at the crowded airport before we could board the plane on our way home. We sat Davis in an empty wheelchair instead of his stroller, and our travel experience immediately shifted. The attendants came to load us up first. We did not stand in line with Davis poking the passenger in front of him. No one eyed us suspiciously as Davis made his sounds of frustration about standing still. People were kinder to him. The wheelchair became the tool by which others could better assess and politely handle our situation. By seating Davis in a wheelchair, others could readily identify and accept that he was different and that he may not display the manners or behavior of other children his age. We had tried to avoid looking different or being a spectacle for so long that the mind shift felt refreshing. We *were* different. Davis deserved to be himself and to be seen as such—without first being misunderstood by others, like Ms. Crotchety—and the wheelchair subtly announced his uniqueness. From that trip forward, we used an airport wheelchair every time we traveled. One day, he would even have a wheelchair of his own.

What we gained from our experience at the family support conference—as well as our travels to and fro—was invaluable. First and foremost, we found a community where we fit. For Rick and me, we were comforted to know that we were not alone in our struggle with PMS and that we could both learn and share our experiences with the other families. While we glimpsed a bit of our future in older 22q children, we also found ourselves providing insight for families with younger 22q kids. For Rick, this was the start of becoming a resource within the PMS community and an advocate for people with disabilities. For me, the sense of purpose I gained from my spontaneous "aha" moment about Doing Davis was a gift. Learning to use a wheelchair was also priceless.

When we returned home from the conference, each of us was different. While Davis could not express how the three days impacted him, his joy at tumbling with others like him had been readily apparent. Rick and I felt less isolated and could talk more openly about disability with one another. For Ryan and Lynnell, the conference was a less positive experience. Perhaps seeing their brother's future made them more fully aware that our family would always deal with Doing Davis. The weekend provided them with a glimpse of what other siblings did with their 22q brother or sister. Feeding them. Taking them back up to their room to have a diaper change. Waiting beside a parent who was doing something for their 22q child. The idea that Davis would never gain independence became frighteningly real for them. In response, they shifted away from the demands of disability and began to fight hard for their own independence.

Despite my initial fears about the conference, I had few regrets in the end. Overall, the conference was an uplifting bonding experience, and Rick and I chose to focus on the positive possibilities for our future running with the herd.

13

NEW HORIZONS

"It is not the mountain we conquer but ourselves."

Edmund Hillary

2001

At our first PMSF conference, Rick maintained a relatively distant demeanor. Other family support group members would later tease him about this, for Rick became very involved in all future conferences. His experience with our local regional center's support services and California's Self-Determination program provided valuable information to other families. Once elected to our town council, he further developed his narrative skills—not that attorneys need much work in that area. In future sessions, he would lead, volunteer, and mentor. We both did. Often, it seemed that we had experience and knowledge to share regarding educational arrangements or institutional support services or even medical conditions that Davis would manifest first (like the arachnoid cysts in his brain). We shared our information and approach to it all as best we could. We shared our educational plans, our state Self-Determination budget for his care, and our medical records.

We discussed the helpfulness of having an Individualized Education Plan, or an IEP, for Davis. Since federal law mandates and provides funding and support for students with learning disabilities, many of the other parents also had feedback about working with an IEP.

From the time Davis entered kindergarten, Rick and I were fortunate to work with a comprehensive team of physical therapists, teachers, administrators, speech or eye specialists, and more each year to craft an IEP that set goals and accomplishments specific to Davis's needs and capacities. Everyone we met and worked with in the school system over the years had a big heart, which was a blessing, and our IEP meetings went smoothly. We were able to ensure that Davis received special education focused on his cognitive capacity while also attending a regular classroom for a part of each day. He was not comfortable in a typical classroom setting for very long, but those interactions provided some special memories. For example, one Halloween, Davis was in a regular class watching a scary movie. At the most intense part, when the room was silent and something spooky happened in the film, Davis laughed, really loud. The rest of the class joined in. I loved hearing these stories about others appreciating a child for his differences.

Another program that was very critical for us was Self-Determination. Rick was instrumental in enrolling us and many others in this program. As he once explained:

California is what is known in the world of developmental disability as "an entitlement state," meaning that those with disabilities are entitled to receive services and supports to assist those with disabilities and their families to live lives like those who are not disabled. Compared to other states, California is generous. However, more than 80% of adults in California who are challenged by developmental disabilities live in poverty. Services and supports allow this underserved group of people to survive. Few thrive.

In 2000, the California Legislature approved a pilot project in which individuals with developmental disabilities were given the freedom to choose their own services and supports, thereby gaining control over their lives. This was a radical departure from the way services and supports were made available to persons who needed them. It was named "Self-Determination." Choice and control were shifted from the state to the consumer and family. The pilot project was to be for a period of three years. Davis was selected as one of only 150 throughout California to participate. The three-year pilot project has continued to this day, an unqualified success.

The reason Self-Determination has continued to this day is largely because Rick, along with other disability advocates, worked hard to promote the state's Self-Determination program so that more might be eligible over the coming decades. Due to their hard work, the state eventually passed legislation to include more individuals, with the hope that in time all 350,000 people with developmental disabilities in California might have the option to receive supports and services through Self-Determination.

In the Self-Determination program, Davis always had a budget, year in, year out. We used it to pay for diapers, a wheelchair, and, later, caregivers. At the end of each year, we often had surplus money in our budget because directly purchasing what we needed was simply more cost-effective than buying things through government vendors and dealing with heaps of bureaucratic paperwork. We returned the leftover balance to the regional center and set up our budget for the following year. The budget always changed based on Davis's changing needs.

After a few years of attending the PMSF conferences, the family support board of directors asked Rick and me to give a presentation together to provide information to new parents.

With Rick's input, I prepared a PowerPoint presentation about our family's experience titled "Doing Davis" to share our story. The presentation began with an ethereal image of hope and dreams as we contemplated the birth of a child. Slide two was "The Big Oops," our child's birth with a genetic deletion. This slide evoked laughter from the audience because they could relate, I supposed. We all had a similar sense of sliding off the cliff into the land of disability. Slide by slide, Rick and I shared our experience of raising a child with physical and intellectual limitations, missing developmental milestones, and missing typical family moments. Rick would lay out the facts on screen. I would emote via microphone. Specifically, Rick pontificated on the institutional and the legal ins and outs of the experience. I spoke of the emotional journey. When teasing Rick, I referred to our combined styles as "Aristotelian Logic meets the intuition of metaphysics."

My goal, in each presentation, was to teach these newer families to train for joy. The sorrow was a given. But our attitude counted. Words mattered, as my buddy Deena, an Olympic Marathon Bronze medal winner, would often remind me.

Rick once described our son as "suffering" from PMS to about fifty people from the Department of Developmental Services in California. I adjusted his word choice during a break. When he returned to the podium, he smiled as he said, "My wife reminds me that our son is challenged by, not suffering from, Phelan-McDermid Syndrome."

Telling our tale allowed us to step into our authentic selves. In the beginning of our experience as parents of a child with special needs, Rick and I purposefully did not share much with family or friends. We did not want to relive our scary moments in hospitals or medical appointments. We wanted to blend in, to be part of a community beyond disability. We hoped that Davis's siblings would be immune from the fragility we felt about Davis and his ability to live. In retrospect, this lack of sharing was a big mistake. We eventually discovered that the touchstone of our unique experience was and would remain disability. What we did not say aloud could become more toxic through silence. We learned this at our very first PMSF conference. As another layer of ignorance peeled away, we shifted. We learned to speak about our experience with disability. We began to openly share our stories, which eventually led to speaking engagements and advocacy for both of us. But it was a slow transition that was still painful at times.

14

THE SAD SOUND OF SILENCE

"I considered my options. There was only one. I
knew. There was always only one. To keep walking."

Cheryl Strayed, *Wild*

2001

We celebrated Davis's sixth birthday in the fall of 2001. A month
later, I received a phone call from my dear friend Sue asking, "Can
you come, now?" Her son, Christopher, who had severe medical
issues and special needs, was dying. She, her husband Bill, and a
group of friends had gathered in Christopher's room in the hospital just blocks away from where we lived, and she wanted Rick and
me to be there.

Sue—the I-Love-Lucy buddy who brought me back to life when I
wanted to hide. The mother who had already lost one child with special needs to a medical condition that her second child Christopher
had as well. She did not know what it was; even genetic testing had
provided no answers. Recently, a feeding tube was placed in his
abdomen after so many years of bottle feeding. He needed more
nourishment, and the feeding tube was the only way for him to get
it. But he pulled it out, and the bleeding could not be stopped.

I listened. I swallowed. I felt numb.

Dying?

How can he be dying?

Christopher, we have navigated through so many medical emergencies together, your mom and me. Why now? I thought our sons were invincible. Are they not?

"I need to get to the hospital," I explained to someone in the Mammoth Lakes Foundation office, where I was preparing a fall writing workshop. I shared that Christopher was in the hospital and Sue had asked me to come and say goodbye. I felt detached from the topic as I spoke, an old trick to keep my eyes dry and pretend all was well in our world.

To say goodbye.

At the hospital, Rick and I stood behind Sue and Bill and alongside many of their other friends around Christopher's bed. The monitors beeped slower and slower. Then the beeping stopped. We gravely bowed our heads in reverence to a brave battle well fought for nine years.

Silence, from a monitor, cannot be described.

We left the room while Sue bathed and prepared her child for the unthinkable. As much as the hospital equipment alarms set off a surge of adrenaline through my body since Davis's birth, their silence was hauntingly worse. The silence held a sadness, a vast, cavernous, ominous absence of life. Like a snuffed-out candle. Gone. Like the soul of her precious son.

The next few weeks, I let myself into Sue's home each morning and brought her a cup of coffee as she soaked in her tub, soaked in her pain. Though Christopher was absent, she continued her routines, morning and night. In the tub, she seemed to hold on to her connection as a caretaker, since she had sat behind her son to bathe him each day. We said very little as she sat in the bath without him, and I stayed nearby in the next room after delivering her coffee. All I could do was to come up alongside her and her grief. By showing up, I tried to encourage her to step forward when she felt ready, as she had done for me over the years. I simply did for Sue what I had learned from her—a friend was someone who kept your heart beating when you ran out of air.

———

About a year after Christopher's passing, Sue and I ventured north to do some shopping in Reno. We drove three hours through winding canyons and small towns to get to the city. We didn't talk much along the way, for my friend was still fragile.

Then, while we were shopping, I pulled out the fart machine. The very one that Sue had given me years before. We placed the battery-operated device beneath a rack of clothes and watched shoppers jump when the raunchy bodily sounds came out from beneath a folded pair of pants. She proceeded to push the button in an elevator and in a checkout line. She pressed the button a lot. Each time, we laughed. We needed to laugh. This is what Sue had taught me from our earliest moments together—humor helps in hard times. If you don't have much around, cultivate it. It is the gift that keeps giving, even when times are tough.

While tending to Sue, I missed some important signals in my own heart and mind. I too was on pause, unable to reconnect. The Christmas season was approaching, but I had no joy. I did not relish decorating our home or our tree. I snuck into the bedroom early each evening to escape into sleep. Had Sue not been grieving, she would have popped my world back open, but neither of us knew that I had also fallen off my happy perch—partly in grief for her loss and partly for fear of losing Davis. I realized all too well that we could lose him. I spiraled downward into depression just as the holidays came around.

15

REMEMBERING OUR ROOTS OF LOVE

"Out beyond ideas of rightdoing and wrongdoing,
there is a field. I'll meet you there."

Jalal al-Din Rumi

2001

I should have been thrilled, proud, happy. Anything but cautious and sad. Our six-year-old son was selected to represent the California special needs community by assisting Governor Davis and his wife, Sharon, in lighting the holiday tree on the State Capitol lawn. The ceremony would be in front of cameras and hundreds of people. Helicopters flew above, and snipers perched atop the building on the roof for post 9/11 security. That was not why I felt empty.

I felt ever so proud of Davis and his moment to shine. But I also felt the weight of sadness from the passing of Christopher and the ever-expanding gap in our home between the rest of my family and me, except for Davis. He became my buffer. When I needed to sit and pause, I sat on the couch with him in my arms and watched the others. They left for school and work. They returned. Lynnell snuggled; the others did not. Davis and I observed, from our place on the couch or a dining room chair, as they cooked or watched television. I had lost the strength to create a meal or initiate an activity. And so I, we, observed.

We drove to Sacramento in two cars because our eldest wanted his own vehicle—away from us. Rick had not touched me that day.

No kind words, not one glance of connection throughout our frenetic race to get to Sacramento, five hours from our home. We had reserved two rooms at the hotel: one for the boys and one for the girls. The girls also had Davis. I lacked the capacity to speak up and engage, to accept the disintegration and the separation, except in silence.

We stopped to shop for dress clothes for the event, and then we hurried to our hotel rooms and made ourselves ready for our rush to the Capitol. Once there, we were guided to a reception where I stood alone with Davis in my arms, and our daughter stood by my parents.

My back began to ache from the weight of Davis in my arms, and I set him down to stand on his own. Within moments he lost his balance and fell. He bonked himself a bit hard and cried with a frustration that I also felt. I did my best to console him. I tried to stand him back up and, as I did, Sharon Davis, the First Lady of California, knelt beside me to help. She became my one heartfelt connection that day, a woman I did not know.

I thanked the First Lady. Someone behind me used a tissue to wipe Davis's nose, then cleaned the smudge from Davis's nose off my shoulder. Startled, I turned. They continued to clean me, wiping my hand just before Governor Davis approached us to shake it. Then everyone left rather quickly.

Rick found us, and we hustled after others heading toward the stage in front of the Capitol. Governor Davis and his wife stepped up to the platform as we rushed across the lawn to our seats beside theirs, half carrying Davis. In the dark, we made our way down the white marble steps of the State Capitol building aiming for a wooden platform set up on the park lawn. An enormous Christmas tree about two stories tall stood beside the impromptu stage. We never did catch up to the procession, but we did find our place near the tree.

I shivered from the dampness of the nearby Sacramento River Delta. I heard our son's name as Rick led him toward the First Couple and the red switch for the tree lights. Flashes from cameras and a steady roar from the helicopters above set my nerves on edge. I heard Davis squeal into the microphone, and the tree lit up. The audience laughed. Davis continued to hit the switch again and again. His smile was as bright as the tree lights. I relaxed. He did it, and he did it well.

When the ceremony ended, we returned to the reception room for more mingling. I watched Davis walk in his wobbly way beside Sharon Davis, waist-high to her, his blonde head brushing against the sleeve of her crisp red silk suit. The Governor's official photographer stepped forward across from us as we surrounded a large table displaying a poster-size greeting card from Davis's kindergarten class. The First Lady bent down to ask him a question. The photographer aimed his camera. Davis spotted the lens and became excited. He loved to pose for people, but he could not understand what the camera did. He knew people's voices became playful when a camera came out, their voices lighter, enticing him to look. The First Lady leaned in toward him for the photo. My son smacked her with a squawk of delight. Cause and effect, his game.

I heard the group around us gasp. I wanted to slide under the linens of the table to hide, but as I met her eyes, which twinkled, I knew she understood. Her compassion and acceptance were much-needed gifts for Davis and me. I thanked her and held onto that moment as an exercise in grace that I could tap into on the many tough days ahead.

———

On Christmas morning, Rick and I set up our movie camera. Lynnell was always first to the tree, chasing gifts with her name and piling them up. Ryan, a teenager, hid his enthusiasm. But Lynnell had plenty of excitement for the two of them and brought presents to Ryan and me that morning.

One of Rick's presents to me was a small, framed print by Paul Nzalamba of an African couple sitting beneath a tree with their backs to one another. Rick included a handwritten card with the gift, which read:

> This picture is called Disagreement. When two people fall in love, it is important that if they ever have a disagreement, they should not see it as the end, but rather as a time to step outside the home to their children. They go to a tree which they planted when they fell in love. Their love has deep roots and has therefore grown into a tree with branches that shelter them. They share the same color, which shows their connection and commitment to each other. Here the man's head is down, as he has some issues to solve within himself, perhaps because his feet are not on the ground. She, on the other hand, is firmly grounded and waits because the tree fits both of them well. On some days, they come here when she is down, and often when neither is down because the tree shelters them and reminds them of their roots in love. Each time they come to this tree, they will find there has been growth, meaning that their love has grown stronger. Let's think of the love we share, the common roots, and the shelter of our tree which will always be there.
>
> Love Rick.

I took in a deep breath and exhaled slowly. The story told of so much more than Rick and me. It spoke to me of how life was defined by before and after. Before when we laughed, with Ryan and Lynnell. And after, when we didn't. I felt clueless when it came to spotting the fault line between doing okay and drowning. I could only stumble across the result that wore me down. We, the Woods, were in trouble. He knew it. I knew it. And the letter placed our knowing front and center.

Ryan finished with his presents and escaped to the homes of his friends. Lynnell played with her gifts. Davis tore apart wrapping paper. Rick and I said little. The challenge of disability, we knew, impacted many families. More than half, we once read, split apart. In the days to follow, I came to understand I was no longer eager for the next part of life to unfold. Rather, I was depressed in the face of the long road of disability that awaited us. I was tired.

I had been avoiding any interaction that might remind me of my pain. In a cave of my own making, I was hiding from the death of my friend's child, the loss of connection to our oldest son, and my inability to reconnect with Rick.

I had found myself in the depths of a similarly dark cave just before I became pregnant with Lynnell. My parents, my siblings, and my in-laws stood back as if depression were contagious. However, I found my footing during the pregnancy, and I stepped up and out. Because I had been there before, I knew I could escape from depression again. It was slow at first. For me, the acknowledgment of what I felt led to opening up the process of healing. I used the third person, a therapy tool I learned earlier. *Cheryl is feeling more than sad. Sinking. A familiar cave.* Next came compassionate self-talk and an affirmation that I was not alone. *Cheryl can do this. She has excellent resources, tools. Many people have felt depleted, empty, unable to step into their day with strength and hope.* I pulled out my journal to share my thoughts with me. As the darkness shifted, I set up a plan, a path for our family in response to that Christmas of darkness.

Doing Davis did not break me that season. But pretending that all else around me was okay did. The mask of a smile had not worked. The world did not smile back. As I pulled back the layers of thought—first the ignorance about being in a depression, then the awareness and sense of shame that I had returned to such a sad, familiar spot—the truth came through.

The truth was that the process of Doing Davis was less challenging than step-parenting a teen, closing down the day as a lonely spouse when Rick was stuck in another town meeting, or hoping for a quiet moment amidst the frenetic energy of my daughter. Doing Davis was relatively easy. Figuring out how to rebuild myself and our family into a beautiful whole would take a little more work.

16

DING

"I am not what happened to me, I am what I
choose to become."

Carl Jung

2002

I longed for a better, more connected version of the Woods and
began to work toward this goal. Rick and I both became more com-
municative, which helped the struggles we had faced over the holidays to dissipate.

Still, we knew we could take nothing for granted. We paid more
attention to one another, listened better, and parked our pride on
the outskirts of our relationship as best we could. We both had more
than we needed.

Meanwhile, I started to question what we lacked, besides time and
the quiet open space in our day to be with each other. Rooms came
to mind. Perhaps if each child had their own space, our time together
in the kitchen and living area might feel easier, lighter, happier?

I also wanted a quieter street. We lived in a neighborhood with a
busy road, and Davis liked to run into the road once I opened the
car door and he could escape my grip. He liked the way I chased
him, the way I screamed at oncoming cars, the way I scooped him
up and carried him back to safety. To him, it was a game. For me,
it was terrifying, even when I managed to stop him before he tore
down the driveway.

After the strain of the holidays, it would have served us well to seek family counseling or couple therapy. Instead, I wanted to look for a new home. Rick agreed.

We swiftly found a home with two cul-de-sacs, one in front of our house and one at the end of the street, two lots away from ours. Dead-end perfect. Davis quickly lost interest in running down the road when he discovered I no longer chased him. *Note to self, chase this fellow when it is safe to do so, he loves it.*

Because we moved away from the school, Davis, six-and-a-half, began to take the bus to school. It was a short yellow bus well known by the parents of children with disabilities. When the bus rounded the bend toward our home, Davis would kick up his heels in his version of a Happy Dance.

His days at school became longer, and I found I had more free time. I hiked when it was warm, skied when it snowed—always with friends. I also wrote in my journal when I found time at the table to relax. I began to have more time for the other children, too, though our oldest was no longer interested in spending much time with the family. He was busy ski racing across the western states. When home, he had friends to see and places to be that did not include parents or siblings.

To avoid the sadness, isolation, and stress I felt as I shared a home with a high school teenager becoming independent, I intentionally approached these tough years differently with Lynnell. I made purposeful time for her apart from Davis while she was in middle school. I drove her to Reno for music lessons because she loved the harp. I drove her to Bishop for horseback riding lessons, and soon she was jumping and had a horse to call her own.

I stretched myself as best I could to accommodate her interests while also taking care of Davis, the family's needs, and creating space for a bit of play for me. It was a balancing act requiring that I pretend the oldest did not snarl, the middle child did not bounce, and the youngest would never again have a medical issue. Also, I tried to ensure that all of us had a piece of Rick's attention. He had become the Mayor of Mammoth Lakes, which required frequent travel to other ski resort towns for comparative analysis, had a thriving law practice, and worked as a statewide advocate for people with disabilities.

During this time, I also developed my writing and penned a few articles for the local newspaper. On one particular day, I was walking by a storefront near Rick's office building when I saw my most recent piece taped onto the window with a big exclamation mark. *Well, paint me proud*, I thought. Someone liked what I had to say and wanted to pass it forward.

AH DA

A small yellow school bus makes its way down our road just as Kapalua finishes her canine dance in the forest and drops her business. I rein her in, meet the bus, and accept my charge with a smile masking my fatigue.

"How was he today?" I ask, hoping Davis did not bite the driver again.

"He was great. Even stayed in his seat," replies the kind bus driver as he eased out from behind the large steering wheel to guide my seven-year-old down the steps safely.

Upon seeing me, my son squeals with excitement. His messages are clipped syllables discernible only to my ears, and I take delight in each.

"Da!" he declares. "Ah da!"

"Yes. All done." His bus ride is over. I brush my hand across his short, coarse blonde hair that does not quite cover the scars on the top of his head and by his left ear. Angry molten red marks reminding me that he survived and that part of our struggle is *ah-da*.

Life for all of us is a series of ah-da's. When we take off his shoes before he wobbles up the stairs to the living room, he is *ah-da* with shoes and socks. When I hug his father, he quickly scrambles between us and declares that we are *ah-da* before yanking one of us off to play.

Even in hospitals, when one of his emergencies has ended, he wearily declares *ah-da* to the doctors and nurses who smile with such deep empathy that my eyes often well up with tears. These medical specialists are witnesses to my son's brave battle to march on to his next *ah-da*. Each night, as I fall into my bed, I begin with my own *ah-da* included in a prayer of thanks for the simple lessons learned and another beautiful day in our mountain home.

Like any busy life, mine consists of a series of lists and piles of incomplete tasks that haunt me when given their due. The quilt I meant to finish. The tax pile I promised to complete early. The thank-you note I never wrote. The attention I pay to these ghosts of incompleteness is exhausting until I return to the philosophy of ah-da.

At any given moment, I look to the task at hand and acknowledge its completion. This morning I packed my special boy's lunch after bathing and diapering him for school. These are my ah-da's. Beside me is a list of not ah-da's, and each will be given its moment, checked off, and acknowledged as time and attention allow. I will not be haunted by guilt or by the decree of others on what is important and what is not. All I have is this moment, and the first item on my list is to complete this small essay about letting go of the pressure to have it all…*ah-da*.

During this same week that "Ah Da" was in the paper, as our Mayor's wife, I played host to the families of Rob Lowe and Kenny G. I gathered friends to retrieve them from an RV that could not get into town due to snow. We delivered them to a beautiful lodge I represented as a realtor that had been for sale. I introduced them to the ski area personnel who managed the security for high-profile visitors to the mountain. One evening, the two couples invited me to share a glass of wine with them. They had read the article I wrote. As curious as I was about them, I found them curious about my experience as Davis's mother. I appreciated their graciousness.

My writing felt important. The words shook out the truth that my smile often denied. In fact, "Ah Da" revealed more about my busyness and over-commitment than I could otherwise admit. I had measured my self-worth by my tangible accomplishments: committee work, chairing a bond measure to bring community college buildings to Mammoth, working on a real estate license, and serving on the board at the Mammoth Lakes Foundation. I had fooled myself into thinking these goals mattered more than my role as a parent, wife, daughter, and friend; that my achievements trumped keeping my family well and strong. I needed to get myself back on a path home to myself and those I cared about. My writing woke me up and stirred up a lot of thoughts.

Could others—the parents of children who require a lifelong commitment like ours—benefit from hearing our stories? Would it help to share how picking up the pen and writing might help them as it had helped me? Could we build a printed page community with opportunities to learn, to listen, to pause, and to be present alongside those born different? Could we create a guide with our words as markers for others to follow in the peculiar land of disability?

Finally, if I wrote Davis's story, could my chapters offer some healing for my fragmented tribe, The Woods?

———

I found a writing buddy, and in the spring of 2004, we slipped off to a writer's retreat on Whidbey Island in the Puget Sound. This trip was my first week away from my family in ten years.

Part of the retreat included a day of silence to stir up the creative juices. Afterward, we were prompted with a writing exercise in which we should ask the characters who would be on paper for permission to write about them. On this day, much to my surprise, I found a voice for Davis—which felt terrific considering he could not speak with words. The imaginary character Lynnell clapped her hands. Imaginary Rick shrugged an okay with his shoulders. Imaginary Ryan walked off the page. Then Imaginary Davis smiled and spoke.

I sat beneath an eave of the roof, watching the rain. The landscape before me vibrated with green and fluorescent yellow made sharp against the drizzle of fog. In a dream-like trance, I met a different version of Davis, this one older.

He strode in with all the fullness of manhood and gifted me his presence. He said thank you for a job well done. He was grateful that I had made my shoulders strong—as the saying goes—for the young to stand upon.

"Yoga," I told him.

"Yes," he answered.

The sky continued to weep as images and thoughts about my connection to Davis and the others in my family unfolded. My pen captured as much as I could without losing the opportunity to be present to the experience.

"Davis," I said to the man in my meditation, "I am not sure how this will all come out. Not sure where you will be." My unspoken fear was that once the story was told about the magic and miracle of Davis, he would leave. He would die.

The tall Whidbey version of Davis took my hand, enclosing it in his, and kissed the inside of my palm. Then he placed our hands together. "I will always be here," he answered, "Right here. In your heart."

I looked away, drew in a breath, and looked back into his brilliant blue eyes.

"Then I guess I should write," I replied, "so I can be here too!"

The next day our class came back together after twenty-four hours of silence. Oddly enough, we remained silent. The experience had seemed to impact us all, whatever our writing, whatever our story.

My experience with the grown-up Davis had been so powerful that I thought I would continue writing about Davis for the next assignment. Instead, I delved into my own story. I felt flawed because I had not had a typical, settled childhood, and I followed this unorthodox start to life with a turbulent set of years through my teen years and well into my twenties. I could fool many people with my outward smile, but in writing, I could not fool myself. The story that flowed from my pen was not what I intended to write that week of exploration.

I titled the story "Ding" for all of the judgments and demerits I had received in life, whether my fault or not. The first ding arrived when a teenage bully enraptured with his newfound manhood stole my precious innocence. I was six. He cornered me when my parents were away. He continued to corner me for years. The shame had been the source of my bulimic pattern. Lynnell arrived on the cusp of a dark depression. Writing and sharing this first of many dings helped me release them, roll them out like stones from the heart, and perhaps create more space for those I loved.

My pen flew across the paper, and the dings poured out. Married and divorced—the first to do so in our family tree. Ding. Pregnant without a spouse. Double ding. A dear friend and fellow renegade, Karen, who understood and adored my dinged-up self asked me to be her maid of honor when she married. She also had a great sense of humor and chose to dress us all in black shoulderless bridesmaids outfits. I was eight months pregnant. The comments were priceless as my broad silhouette faced my buddy during the ceremony, without a ring on my own finger.

But apart from a few who understood me, and called me CJ, I had to make some hard choices about blending in or phasing away. In voicing the experience of my six-year-old self, I had a choice. To own my truth or that of my family. For them it never happened. To have spoken its impact on me as a child was yet another big ding best swept under the rug.

Eyes on my life would have thought I moved forward as I received honors in high school, college, and graduate school. There were special political and corporate internships. But as I studied and worked, I wandered like a gypsy and could not stay in one place for long. My siblings married, settled down, and established careers. I continued the search for Don Quixote's darn "Impossible Dream," no matter how hopeless. For each transgression, each choice down a path less followed, I received a ding, whether purposeful or unconsciously assigned by some members of my family of origin. I accepted each ding as my fault.

While writing "Ding," I recognized the grip of such judgment on my psyche, on my soul, and let it go as I shared my tale. I discovered that my experiences supporting Davis had grown me up because he loved me so fully and depended on me so exclusively. I could find my own affirmations about my soul and my past.

Life had been ding, ding, ding. And then along came Davis. And the dings shifted their tune.

What I had overlooked—until I packed the dings together in one hard, honest, exhausting synopsis during that writing retreat—was that the uniqueness of my experiences had made me a better woman, a stronger person, a special being. And I was just like everyone else. Everyone made good choices and poor ones. Everyone had a bully in their life. Everyone had a mentor. Everyone had a challenge. As different and flawed as I was to the very bottom timbre of my dings, I blended in with the rest of humanity because a ding has many tones.

A friend from our writing circle walked up to me the next day with a gift wrapped in a blue scarf. I opened the scarf and cried. She had presented me with Tibetan bells called *tingshas*, used for healing, praying, clearing negative energy, and restoring harmony and balance. A leather strap connected the disks. When struck together, the tingshas created a clear resonant sound, a ring.

"So you can create a more beautiful ding," she shared.

When I next contemplated the word "flawed," I found beauty in its individuality. The non-apologetic possibility that "different" was in no way "flawed." Acceptance of paths less traveled, acceptance of messages that stirred discomfort, and acceptance of what feels dissonant and different helps broaden our mindsets. The opportunity to be more of the person I saw in my writing and when I was with close friends blossomed. I felt pushed past my comfort zone, and rather than feeling fear, I felt exhilarated. As it turned out, I deserved my own love, as we all do. Davis had been instrumental in teaching me to get over myself. He adored me, flaws and all—and that was all that I needed.

17

FROZEN NANNY

"Trust starts with truth and ends with truth."

Santosh Kalwar

2004

My week on Whidbey Island was possible because we had consistent help for Davis after school—often from his one-on-one aides from school. Nonetheless, letting go and trusting others came slowly for me, particularly because of a bad experience when Davis was about five.

A woman we hired wanted to take him to her home to watch him. In the weeks that followed, Davis began to act out at home by crying more and needing more attention. He also began to bang his head in frustration. We received a call from one of her neighbors, who warned us that Davis's caretaker was neglecting him. The caretaker assured us all was well and that the call was from a neighbor that she did not get along with. Quick note: Trust your gut! For some reason, we didn't.

I had been spending my time away from Davis preparing a writing workshop. The preparations involved hiring the instructors, getting the word out to the local community of writers and visitors, and making sure we had the budget and location for the event.

The evening before the workshop, I was at a dinner with the instructors. A friend came by our table, and I said, "Hello."

"No," she said. "It's Davis. We need to go."

I was up and out of my seat and into her car in a moment. We headed straight to the emergency room. All she could tell me was Rick had carried Davis into the ER bleeding from his head, with Lynnell trailing behind. She and her husband had grabbed Lynnell so she would not be in the room with the emergency. Then she came to get me. By the time we arrived at the ER, the crisis was explained.

Davis had been isolated in the back when Rick arrived at the caretaker's home. As Rick touched his bangs, Davis's head began to bleed from a recent stitch location. (The stitches had been the result of tumbling into a door frame). In that backroom where the caretaker had isolated Davis, he had been banging his head against the wall. He re-opened the wound and needed new stitches. Head wounds bleed profusely, and Rick immediately reacted to the gushing blood. Once the emergency was over, we confronted the caretaker and talked with her neighbors. We pieced together a story of horrific neglect, including being left in a car while she was inside doing other tasks.

I felt awful. Davis had been so unhappy and unable to do more than bang his head to tell us. It took me a year to peel my fingers off my boy—a year. During that year, Rick became the only person I trusted with Davis when I needed a break.

Still, breaks were necessary, and we slowly found babysitters with good hearts. Our regional center provided "respite money" to pay others to give parents these breaks. When Rick helped us get into the Self-Determination program, a big part of our budget was for outside help.

Our situation was in no way unique. It was often the case that as the needs of a disabled child became more acute, one parent became the primary caretaker, with the flexibility to manage the medical appointments and hospital stays. The other parent became the primary income earner to compensate for the decrease in family income and to meet the increase in expenses related to disability. Hiring help was expensive. Some parents took on the full-time role of caretaker for their child with special needs, but I was not one of them. When the children were young, I wanted to watch Ryan ski in his races and take Lynnell away from home for an adventure that did not include everyone else. Back then, we had babysitters for a few hours here and there but with no set schedule.

Finding a person with the compassion to caretake was the tricky part, and though we had many amazing caretakers, we also had awful ones.

When Davis was nine, Rick and I decided that perhaps it was time to hire a live-in person to be there and provide a little coverage that would allow us to have a little more spontaneity. We placed an ad in the local paper for a live-in nanny. Because I worked a haphazard schedule in real estate, and Rick's court calendar prevented him from being home when Davis was sick, we opted for hiring another version of me.

To place an ad and ask a stranger into our lives was not easy for us. We decided to test the new person out on our dog, cat, and bird while we were away with Davis on vacation. We hired a potential live-in nanny after checking her references in October of 2004.

"Cheryl," Rick greeted me after his day at the top of the stairs near the kitchen. He wore his lawyer look. Something was up.

"Yes…" I answered.

"I called to tell Nanny she could have the job, and I think she was drunk."

I felt sure that he was overreacting. I gathered more information and decided to drive over to talk to her the next day before we left. I asked her about the possibility that she had been drunk in the afternoon on the previous day. She explained that she was on pain pills for a sprained ankle. She said it had been her last day of pain pills, and she would be fine to watch our animals and our home. That made sense to me.

We gave her the keys to the house and the Suburban. Rick handed our neighbor, Bill, a paper with his cell phone written down along with the place we would be staying. Just in case.

You never know.

What could go wrong?

We received a call from Bill on the last day of our trip.

"There's been an incident," he said.

Bill routinely walked his dogs morning and night, much like we did. We often crossed paths as we led our canines to the forest to do their business. The night before, a strong early-season snowstorm had hit the Sierra. When he took his dogs for their walk, Bill noticed that the Suburban was parked crookedly in the driveway with the back passenger door open and the interior light on. However, he saw through the upper front windows of the house that the lights were on, the television was blasting, and he assumed that our pet sitter and future nanny was inside and perhaps unloading the car. Snowfall by this point was about six inches or more, and it was very dark. The next morning Bill took his dogs out once again, and as he looked across the street to our home, he noticed that the car was still in the same position with the door open. He thought this was odd. He walked over, moving through what was by then two feet of snow in the early morning light.

He saw a log in the driveway. Curious, he walked toward it and became concerned about its shape. As he brushed off some snow, he touched a bare leg with his hand. It was cold as ice and looked almost like marble. He ran home to tell his wife to call 911 and returned to help the frozen nanny. One of the paramedics who responded to the call was a friend of ours and described the state of the nanny. Her limbs were frozen along with part of her cheek, which had been lying against the ground, and he said they thought they were preparing her as an organ donor because they could get no response.

We returned home on our flight and drove back to Mammoth, unsure if the nanny was alive or dead. We learned on the drive back that with the storm still raging, a life-flight for the woman was not an option. An ambulance tried to transport her to Reno, but they were turned back an hour into the drive. All roads north were closed. Somehow though, because of what she had consumed and passed out from, this woman lived. She became a case study for surviving in freezing conditions.

Her trick?

Percocet and alcohol, lots and lots of alcohol. As Rick had suspected, our nanny had a drinking problem after all. And yet, the amount of alcohol in her blood is what saved her life.

———

For me, one of the most complicated parts of disability was caretaking—because I was inherently a caretaker, but we also had to hire caretakers so that I could be *me* and we could be *us*. Rick and I considered ourselves better than anyone we hired, but our after-school caretakers taught us that our way was not always the best way for our son.

I tended to be over-protective, minimizing Davis's opportunity for getting out in the world. Rick often challenged Davis to do more physically and to tolerate more to expand his comfort zone. Thanks to their different perspectives and approaches, our hired care providers created new and better habits for our son simply because we didn't train them to do everything "our way."

I was lucky we had so many people around who loved our son—
and he loved them back. I could tell when he reached for their hand
as easily as he reached for ours. His eyes followed them as they stood
up or walked about. Beneath those blue eyes was a broad smile.
Sometimes, when he stood up to greet them, he did his Happy Dance.

"Ya, ya ya ya."

We hear ya, Davis, I would think.

Rick and I realized that as much as it is a labor of love for parents, caretaking a child or adult with special needs requires an
extra special commitment by those who choose to help. Wages are
low, competition for caretakers is intense, and opportunities for
advancement are limited. So, Rick and I learned to follow "the 90
percent rule," which is that if a caretaker is 90 percent as good as a
child's parent, it is enough.

In this way, Rick and I would continue to hire and monitor the
many people in charge of keeping our son happy and healthy. Yet,
there was no right way to find help. And help was not permanent.
This reality would follow Davis forever. Frozen nannies or not.

18

SHUNT FUNK

"Any idiot can face a crisis—it's the day to day
living that wears you out."

Anton Chekhov

2004

I awoke into a nightmare.

Davis had been sleeping beside me in our bed these past few days.
After a recent shunt replacement surgery, I hated to sleep away from
him. The procedure seemed to have gone well, and we were home
after only one day of recovery in the hospital. Once home, Rick had
to leave town on mayoral business. I unfolded my arm in the dark,
and it brushed against Davis's pillow.

That's wet. I paused.

Turning on the light, I found a halo of moisture around my son's
head. Fluid was leaking from the incision in the back of his head,
where the shunt had been replaced.

Brain fluid. Crap. Holy crap. Okay. Think, think, think.

Breathe.

"Oh Davis," his eyes opened as I whispered, which I often did when
creeping toward the acknowledgment of a crisis. "You look so sad.
Are you hurting, buddy?"

I hated being alone when some part of Davis needed fixing. I
slipped my hand gently behind his head. I felt the bristle of the hair

growing back after having been shaved for surgery a week ago. I felt the long incision. Clear fluid covered my hand.

Oh, crap.

I watched as the fluid trickled onto his pillow. *Double crap.*

Slowly, I made my way off the bed. His eyes followed me. I grabbed a backpack and pulled out my toothbrush, toothpaste, hairbrush, ponytail binders, a book from my nightstand, comfy clothes to wear, and something to sleep in. I packed two extra sets of clothing for myself. My backpack resembled an overstuffed pillow. I walked down the stairs to Davis's bedroom and pulled out diapers, a DVD player, DVDs, shirts and pants, and his toothbrush. From the kitchen, I grabbed a few water bottles. These went into a square bag that also held my laptop. I checked on Davis, who remained quiet, and ran the bags out to the car.

What am I missing? Oh yeah, Advil. Sitting around in hospital rooms seemed to get to my back.

By the time I returned to Davis, the wet halo loomed bigger on the pillow around his head. I helped him up, and we managed our way down two flights of stairs to the car. I was grateful that he was small and I could hold him when he stumbled

At the Mammoth Hospital, an x-ray revealed the problem. The tube to the shunt had fallen into his belly and was no longer attached to the mechanism in his head.

Thus, seepage.

I closed my eyes and sighed as familiar lyrics rang out in my head:

> *Hello Crisis, my old friend*
> *We've come to visit you again.*

Not quite the way Simon and Garfield had intended, but my lyrics often followed my panics.

The shunt could not be fixed in Mammoth, so I had to drive Davis six and a half hours south to his neurosurgeon in San Diego. We were both exhausted by the time we got to the hospital. Our medical team there had found a room and bed for Davis on one of the upper floors; I parked myself for the night beside him in a hard-backed chair.

The next morning a surgeon attached a new tube to the shunt. This tube ran just under the skin over Davis's right shoulder and down into his belly, also called the peritoneum. The doctors opted to leave the old tube where it was, assuming it would not cause problems. We drove back to Mammoth a few days later.

As the days passed and I prepared for Christmas, I was only too aware that my son did not bounce back from this last surgery. I wrapped presents, fixed meals, declined holiday party invitations, and waited for him to get better.

The older children came home from their schools. Ryan was in college, and Lynnell was in a private high school down south. Lynnell needed a quieter place to learn with stronger academics than our small town could provide. We hated that she was gone, but we had decided that the chaos of living alongside Davis was not conducive to her learning.

After the holidays were over and the children returned to school, I waited for Davis to return to his former self. Instead, he stared sadly at us from his place on the couch. When we had to move him, he showed us where it hurt. His eating was a fraction of normal. Still, he never had a fever, and we hoped it was simply a situation that required more time to heal. After long weeks with no real sign of recovery, however, we knew something was very seriously wrong and that we needed to take Davis to the hospital.

A severe winter snowstorm had shut down the roads and airports, but we managed to four-wheel drive our way to our local hospital with Davis. The doctors and Rick and I all agreed that the tube in Davis's belly must be causing his discomfort and decline. We needed to get him back down to his specialists in San Diego once there was a break in the blizzard pummeling the Sierra. The next day, a small gap between storms provided an opportunity to life-flight Davis to San Diego. I packed a bag, and we drove to the Mammoth Hospital, where Dr. Johnson was waiting for us in the parking lot.

His blue eyes met mine. I hugged him. He hugged me back.

When Davis was small and too fragile to make it to the hospital to be checked on as a toddler, Dr. Johnson had come to our home—even in the middle of winter. I have an enduring image of him leaving our house in a whiteout one time. He was truly a saint. He patiently explained confusing medical jargon to help us understand what was happening with our boy, and, in time, the medical terms had become less frightening.

That morning, I again absorbed enough of his calming influence to feel hopeful that Davis and I would be home soon.

"He'll be alright, Cheryl," he assured me as he helped both of us get into the ambulance.

With snow swirling all around, we were taken by ambulance down to the Bishop airport to meet the life-flight. Davis moved very little, barely opening his eyes. The plane took off, and immediately we hit turbulence. We dropped and climbed to get above the storm like a ball bouncing on a wave. On one steep drop, Davis's arms flew out from beneath the sheets, and he tried to sit up, yelping in pain. I sang to him, pretending we were fine. Always fine.

An ambulance met us on the other end of the flight and delivered Davis to the ER—but it took seven and a half hours before Davis and I were given a private hospital room smelling of old air conditioning ducts and antiseptic.

Once Davis was settled in, the staff informed me that a doctor would be by in the morning. In my mind, this was not a satisfactory response to our emergency.

By the next day, after no doctor appeared, I was having a tantrum.

Davis had not eaten in days. He had been throwing up, and bile was all that came out. He was nine and a half years old. He had lost eight pounds and carried only sixty-four. The shunt had been replaced three weeks ago, and he still was not himself. The tube replacement at that time had left another tube in his belly. His belly hurt. I wanted answers, and I wanted someone to fix my boy.

I threatened to carry Davis back down to the ER if they did not have a doctor in his room that day. Finally, someone called in the gastrointestinal crew.

"Peritonitis—a life-threatening abdominal infection," they proclaimed.

On day three, I anxiously paced the hallways while Davis underwent surgery to remove the tubes in his body. The doctors installed an exterior shunt to allow the infection to heal. By early afternoon, Davis was sedated and sleeping in the bed beside my chair. A tube ran from every orifice, including the new one for his exterior brain shunt. I stared at a long new incision that crossed his tummy in an angry red battle line.

On day four, I set up our morning ritual. This grounded me. Ritual always had. I shook out my hips, which were numb from the sleeping chair, turned on Davis's television, and tried to coax a smile from him. Then I searched for coffee. Davis could not yet eat and gagged at the sight or smell of food. His nutrition came from tubes as he recovered.

Day five I dubbed "Groundhog Day" because every day was so much the same until, on day twelve, surgery to replace the tube in his head was scheduled for noon.

Pre-surgery, a nurse took Davis's blood pressure and temperature. The nurse came up with 99.7 °F under the arm. Then a rectal thermometer read 101.5 °F. We tried the mouth. The number climbed. Within three hours Davis's temperature hit 105.2 °F. I barked orders for ice, a pediatrician, and answers.

Davis was miserable. The doctor added morphine, and Davis settled. After Motrin, the fever finally began a steady descent. The pediatrician eliminated such culprits as a brain fluid infection. The doctors suggested that Davis had a rare infection from the peripherally inserted central catheter (PICC) line.

Of course, it was rare, I thought miserably. *Poor boy.*

Day forty-eleven. Or thirty-twenty-one. No, fifty-one. Each morning spilled into the next, and each night slipped by too quickly.

Finally, Davis was scheduled for a surgery that would place another tube from the brain shunt into his heart. His belly could not receive the drainage for another year as it healed from the infection.

His heart?

Everything they touched on my boy seemed to break or never to be the same again.

What about his heart?

Thankfully, the second surgery had no complications, except that I was exhausted. We were finally allowed to go home.

Once home, Davis and I each settled into our beds beneath warm comforters. I listened through a baby monitor to his steady, soft snore.

At eight that evening, Rick returned from a tough, day-long deposition. He did not want to alarm me, but his left arm had shooting pains, and he was short of breath. I could not drive him to the emergency room because we could not leave Davis. Nor could we take Davis because he was too weak. So, Rick drove himself to the hospital to see if his heart was okay. He stayed overnight for observation at the hospital, and fortunately, all of his tests came out fine.

Nevertheless, I noticed that more grey had snuck into Rick's hair while Davis and I were away in San Diego. And each of us started the day more fatigued. Then it became worse.

19

A LIFE FULL OF FLIES

"We must get rid of the life we had planned so as to have the life that is waiting for us."

Joseph Campbell

2007

When Davis turned twelve, he presented us with new challenges. Seizures. Medications. Split lips from a fall. Stitches, so many stitches. A broken arm.

Davis's first classroom aid, Cassie, was with him when he broke his arm during summer school as he fell during a seizure. She was brave and extraordinarily kind. She tended to his safety during a seizure with the same focus Rick and I always did. When Davis fell forward as he was seizing, his arm crumpled beneath him, and amidst the turmoil of the incident, no one knew he had broken his arm.

When I picked Davis up after school that day, he acted sad and whined unusually. Once home, we took him to his chair, and he screamed when he eased himself onto it. That's when I knew something was wrong. I drove Davis to the hospital, and we discovered that he had broken his left arm in the fall. Poor guy couldn't tell us. He spent the rest of the summer out of the water, in a cast. Lymphedema set in, and his left arm ballooned out in a familiar pattern, like his feet, never to return to normal.

Rick and I did what we have always done when it comes to life alongside Davis: we adjusted. It was our son who bore the burden of the brain storms. The least we could do was comfort him through his seizures and later work through the anguish that any parent feels as their child suffers. After each seizure, Davis would sleep, and I would weep. Waiting. Anticipating.

Suddenly one night, the baby monitor next to my bed crackled as sounds emerged, breaking the quiet of night and pulling me up from my dreams. I reached to turn up the volume and heard a long groan broken up by gasps. Fear gripped my heart, yet my mind clicked into action.

"Rick," I pushed my right hand firmly against his warm back as I left our bed. "Davis is having a seizure." I grabbed my terry cotton robe and moved quickly down the stairs from our bedroom loft to Davis's bedroom below.

Our boy stared forward with vacant eyes. His body lay frozen beneath his comforter, his neck and back arched. The groans stopped, and Davis's breath disappeared, hiding, until the next phase of the event. I gently lifted his head and slipped my legs beneath him, cradling him while we waited. With a cadence designed to keep my breath constant, I started to sing. Rick stood near Davis's feet and stared at his watch. He'd had the good sense to grab it off the bathroom counter. We always timed Davis's seizures and knew that if too much time passed, we would call 911.

"I know an old lady who swallowed a fly," I sang. "I don't know why she swallowed the fly. Perhaps she'll *die*," I choked on this last word.

In better times, Davis chuckled when I raised my voice in exclamation. Perhaps he found the inflection of my vocals entertaining, or perhaps his simple mind grasped the absurdity of the scenario as the lady proceeded to swallow more and more of the barnyard to catch that first piece of discomfort.

Rick marked the slow passage of time on his watch. "Come on, baby," he murmured.

"I know an old lady who swallowed a spider, that wriggled and jig-gled and tickled inside her..."

Soon, as the story went, the lady swallowed a bird to catch the spider intended to catch that original bothersome fly. Davis's lips remained still and blue.

Our dog Lucy rested her chin on his legs. Her brown eyes kept vigil over her charge. "Good snuggle, Lucy," I told her, for she was still in training to become Davis's service dog. Her expression seemed to show bewilderment and concern.

"Coming up on a minute," Rick announced while stroking our fro-zen son on his thigh.

A quilt covered Davis, one of the first I ever made. The pattern did not turn out right because I accidentally omitted a row of strips and boxes that played an important role in the total theme. I kept the quilt near Davis because he too was missing a row of bits and pieces that would have created a different boy had they not gone missing.

"I know an old lady who swallowed a dog. Oh, what a hog to swal-low a dog." On we went as time passed. "She swallowed the dog to catch the cat...."

Breathe, Davis. Breathe.

Finally came the long, slow expulsion of his breath. His eyes remained unfocused, but his lean body slid off from the former stiff arched pose. Phase two brought on the twitching and body convulsions.

We waited, whispering encouragement in his ear. Rick stared at his watch. "A minute and a half." The body beneath the comforter stopped twitching, gradually, and then came the stillness of exhaustion.

Davis looked up into our faces, his blue eyes shifting their gaze between Mom and Dad with a look of sadness and fatigue. I wondered what he could comprehend about the hot electric storms that fired up in his brain.

Our dog made her way up and onto the bed to nestle in beside Davis's feet. My son reached for me. We sat together, my arms locking him onto my chest while his short, blonde hair brushed against my cheek. Together we leaned into the pillow. He felt warm, too warm.

"Tylenol," I suggested to Rick as I gently stroked Davis's head. "This feels like something coming on."

Rick returned from Davis's bathroom with red liquid in a spoon.

Early on in his seizures, we did not know that it was not advisable to provide anything to eat or drink because persons with epilepsy could accidentally inhale food or liquid into their lungs in a seizure spasm. We soon mastered what to do and what not to do when Davis had seizures. We learned not to give him food or water, not to perform CPR with my mouth over his even though his lips looked blue, and to never shift him during a spasm (because we could break or injure some part of him). Instead, we learned to pad his world during the early phases of the seizures.

Rick held the spoon up to Davis's mouth. "Here, pal."

Davis complied. He always complied and opened his mouth when we offered him medicine. Whether the spoon contained antibiotics, seizure pills tucked into applesauce, or his pain medication, Davis opened his mouth and accepted what came his way. Luckily, in this instance, ignorantly serving him Tylenol did not cause further problems.

I often wished I could accept whatever came my way with as much grace as my son. I was one of a million moms tending to a child with severe medical issues, one of a million caretakers wishing that I could plan a day without wondering if a medical emergency might interfere. So many of us were tending to butts, wiping and diapering tushes bigger than our own, and huddling alongside our wards in hospitals or waiting rooms.

As I became a better version of myself, I did not wonder "Why me?" so much. Instead, I adopted a "Why not me?" attitude that I learned from other parents and therapists who helped us navigate the strange path of disability.

Around this time, as I processed my life journey, I began to draw labyrinths. I painted one with the colors of the seven chakras. I decided I was in the labyrinth of disability. I was not lost, just making my way through the twists and turns. Then I pondered, *What do I do with that?*

I decided that I could leave a trail behind me so that others might be able to learn from my journey. I became a regional representative for our genetic deletion support group and began fielding calls from new PMSF mothers. They would often call me when they first received what they believed to be a catastrophic diagnosis for their child.

"How do you do it?" they often asked.

I listened; I heard their pain. I had walked along those same forlorn shores wondering how to get back to familiar terrain—life without disability. Many were not yet ready to hear that the tides would pull them further from what they knew.

Just as in the *Welcome to Holland* essay, disability was not what we had planned for as we awaited the birth of our children. Yet my original resistance to life alongside disability had dissipated. I gradually accepted that Holland was where we were. To think that Italy was still an option drained me of my strength and capacity to create the best life possible for Davis, my family, and myself. No one forced us to face the tulips with a new appreciation. We came to our place in our way.

I was careful of what information I passed along. Familiar to the pain of the voyage, I tried to gauge each parent's level of acceptance and denial because, for me, each balanced against the other at various stages in the journey through the topsy-turvy arena of special needs.

"What will this be like?" some asked.

I wanted to say, "Ubiquitous, so much the same, and for so many years." I could not even offer up our family's unique and sometimes twisted Monty-Python-style version of adapting to life alongside Davis with our gallows humor until I understood what they were really asking for. Support? A heart alongside their own to hear their sadness? Or tools?

The Buddhist parable of the second arrow offers a lesson in dealing with suffering. It was said the Buddha once asked a student, "If an arrow strikes a person, is it painful? If a second arrow strikes the person, is it even more painful?" He then went on to explain, "In life, we can't always control the first arrow. However, the second arrow is our reaction to the first. This second arrow is optional."

There is pain with disability. There is grace in acceptance and the will to continue to create a sense of fulfillment and purpose in what we chose for our life. Many did not have such choices. I wanted to be grateful that we, as a family, did.

Some parents faced with a disability wanted, as Rick had, to fix what they could as early as they could. They begged to know the therapies, the nutritional components, and the options to help their child become all they could be. I talked to some parents who were already exhausted when their child was not yet one year old.

I sometimes shared what Rick said at the end of his first marathon in Honolulu. When he finished his time as Mayor, from 2001 to 2006, I thought we might have more open space in our days. Then

Rick decided to run a marathon. He worked with a renowned running coach, Andrew Kastor, based in our town who created a marathon training plan beginning eleven months before a scheduled marathon. Wisely, the plan went out only a month at a time.

Rick said later, "Had I seen the total weekly training mileage in the beginning, I would have quit then and there."

The mileage and commitment were intense toward the end, but he didn't quit. Rick went on to run one or two marathons every year, often earning a podium medal in his age group. Rick equated this slow unveiling of what was ahead to adjusting to seizures.

Davis's seizures started when he was twelve. We sort of got used to them, although you never really do. If we had known then, early on, how many there would be and how devastating they would become, we would have given in to despair.

Instead, we were introduced to seizures one at a time, and we responded, one at a time. When we thought of how difficult seizures were for us to witness as parents, we would remember that it was Davis who time and again demonstrated courage and grit to get through them, one at a time. That was how he did it. He showed us we could persevere too. Similarly, too much information could sink a parent who was new to our world.

When the circumstances of a call allowed for it, I shared that these cherubs came with a silver lining. My son's smile beckoned even the grumpiest of those we met to smile back.

When a parent felt guilty about getting angry or tired out, I shared my own shortcomings. Like the old lady gulping down one quick solution after another to chase her original discomfort, I too swallowed a barnyard and ended up with a bellyache. Sometimes I would reach for a quick fix, like hard, biting words to fight off what I did not want to hear. Sometimes I tuned out to television after a few hours in the ER with Davis. Sometimes food fed my sadness. In the years to come, I added a glass or two of wine to settle myself, forgetting that alcohol is a depressant. But who needed more of that to squelch a darn fly?

One of the first pieces of advice I gave to the new moms after a few calls was "to settle in with the fly." Of course, I did not say "fly." Instead, I encouraged them to be tough enough to cry and silly enough to laugh, eventually, about the same event. I told them that humor helps ease anxiety. I told them stories about my own experiences alongside disability. And I told them that, for me, adapting to a life dedicated to Davis involved acknowledgment and release. My process for this involved meditation in the wee hours of dawn. After that, I would write or draw one of my many bothersome "flies" in a blank journal with colorful pens and pictures. I connected to all that I felt—the pain, the joy, the sweet respite in between—and I allowed myself to acknowledge what my mind or perhaps my soul beckoned me to see.

I tried to share that I had learned to become real cozy with the fly—and that this was not necessarily a bad thing.

One of my favorite Joseph Campbell quotes invites us to "let go of the life you have planned, so as to accept the one that is waiting for you." For the parents of children with disabilities, our destiny—for better or for worse—is a life full of flies.

Happy Holidays 2007

What would the crush of Christmas Mail be like without a recap from The Woods? As our oldest once bemoaned, there is always so much going on. Perhaps that is why we try to fit Maui into our year as often as we can, for the quiet, the space, and the opportunity to reflect on how very blessed both Rick and I feel when we pull up our feet to rest a while.

Speaking of feet, Rick decided to fill what would have been a bit too much space in his schedule after retiring from politics. So, he trained for a Marathon. Leave it to Rick to take it all the way. He trained with an inspiring young man, Andrew Kastor, who happens to be married to Olympian Deena Kastor. Rick decided to qualify for the Boston Marathon on his first go-around. In September at the Maui Half-Marathon, Rick came in twenty-ninth in a field of 1,300. In December he crossed the Oahu Marathon finish line in the top one percent of the pack with a time of 3:28. We're off to Boston in April (I be da masseuse).

Not to be outdone by his dad, Ryan put his feet to the asphalt and with only three weeks of training ran an impressive 10K. (You may recall that Ryan severely injured his right knee while shushing down the hill at over seventy miles-an-hour in the Junior Olympics.) After graduating from UC Santa Barbara this year Ryan filled out his law school applications for the Fall of 2008 and returned to his first love, skiing, in the interim. He is a race coach up at the mountain and leaves this house each day with the biggest smile I have ever seen on his sunburned face.

Our middle one, Lynnell, recently entertained us and her entire school with her Senior Chapel talk. She admitted to being boy crazy and waved to her "boys" in the back who cheered. Regarding her feet, she looked at her parents from the podium once she crossed the stage to say, "Look, I didn't trip!" The event felt like a celebration of her unbridled enthusiasm. Lynnell follows many passions: harp and piano, art, writing, horses, literature, and French, all of which she can pursue in the fall when she ventures off to Smith College on the East coast in 2008.

Well, the youngest continues to keep us on our toes. Davis is healthy as ever but bigger and far more vocal than in his earlier years. He has his own aide in the classroom and works his way into the hearts of so many in our community. Almost everyone we bump into has a Davis Tale to share. Davis also has a new companion, a labradoodle named Lucy that I am training as his seizure service dog. We try not to say "oodle" around Rick who still twitches at the thought of a curly brown-haired dog in the house. When I am not in San Diego training Lucy I try to fit in my work: real estate, and my passions: writing, running, skiing, lunching with the gals, art quilts, and other needlecrafts… oh, and time with the family.

Love from The Woods
Rick, Cheryl, Ryan, Lynnell, Davis, and the pets—little Lucy and our black cat Mystic who is adjusting as best she can with just a few hissing fits.

20

MOM TROT

"I long to accomplish a great and noble task, but
it is my chief duty to accomplish small tasks as if
they were great and noble."

Helen Keller

2008

In the late fall of 2008, I joined a pack of 11,000 runners in the San Jose Half-Marathon. To do this meant planning Davis's care while we were away and hoping he had no health issues arise both before and during our absence. Timing, planning, and hoping were key to any getaway. Over the years, Doing Davis had trained me to be open to adjusting to changed plans. In this case, I was able to run my race.

During the race, I measured my progress by my watch and the mile markers. My pace held steady—not fast, just steady. I ran to reach the other side. Other marathon runners, like my husband, ran to set a new personal record or PR. My PR was just showing up and finishing.

Many of the runners became familiar faces after the halfway mark. I followed one young woman with a bouncing ponytail for a few miles near the end as we wove our way in and out of the business district toward the finish line. Then she stopped, ahead of me, seemingly exhausted. She began to walk. I came up behind her and tapped her on her shoulder.

"Come on!" I said.

She did. When she caught her breath, we chatted a bit, but not much because both of us were tired. Her first words included a thank you. Then she kept running, and we finished close together, with me on her heels.

Afterward, I reflected that my tap on her shoulder was not only what runners did, but what many amazing people did for me: we all encouraged each other to go on. We all supported one another to get to where we needed to be, together.

Each PMSF bi-annual conference allowed Rick and me and the other parents to learn from one another and mentor one another. By sharing our stories, we helped "tap" each other forward in our marathons of caretaking.

Our community in Mammoth Lakes shared encouraging taps by fundraising when someone was in need or delivering food or kind words when needed. We had a great team of teachers, doctors, and therapists who helped us continually move forward. We also benefited from the Disabled Sports Eastern Sierra program (DSES), which paired volunteers to ski or ride bikes with our different-ly-abled community members. Davis especially loved participating in this program over the years.

Through interacting with these supportive groups, I learned that we grow as we give, as we listen, and as we share our stories around "challenge." Sharing my stories about Davis was intended to be a tap for other parents.

In my writing, I strove to convey both the easy moments with Davis and his difficult phases. I related how his Happy Dance was an expression of pure joy and how pain or sadness evoked his tears. I had so many stories—like when eight-year-old Davis streaked through a town business cocktail party in our home during his clothes-off phase. Everyone had laughed. These were the light-hearted tension-breaker moments that juxtaposed against the angst and heartbreak of watching as paramedics whisked him into an ambulance in so many other instances. For me, safe grace felt like somewhere in the middle, between joy and sorrow.

Back to the reason I do not run in a 5K, 10K, half-marathon, or marathon for the best time? Because I prefer to run the race the way I caretake Davis: not for a personal record or a place on a podium. Rather, for the simple pleasure of laying my head on my pillow at the end of the day and mentally noting three things I am thankful for on that day. My "three gratitudes" are always unique to the day, the place I am in, and the people around me. As I go to bed, feeling thankful helps me to sleep better. A day closes. Not won. Just done. And grateful.

21

DO ALL, BE ALL

"If you try to change it, you will ruin it. Try to hold
it, and you will lose it."

Lao Tzu, *Tao Te Ching*

2009

The only constants to Doing Davis seemed to involve continually
adjusting to new truths about what our son would never be able
to do and finding help. I had a wonderful care provider named
Guillermina who took Davis into her home with other children
when he was small. Later she helped us by babysitting on weekend
date nights. Her family became his other family. Though I thought
that I could do it all, I needed another caretaker so that I could have
time to be *me*. I needed a gentle tap to remind me that Davis was
the all I could do when it came to caretaking. I discovered this on
Christmas Eve in the winter of 2009.

I was in the kitchen preparing the holiday dinner for my extended
family when I heard a faint groan. Instinctively I looked toward
Davis. He was in the corner of the living room, clapping to his television show. My mother was missing. I ran down the flight of stairs
from our living room to the garage and threw open the door.

Mom lay prone on the cement floor, not moving but groaning.
She had fallen. Hard.

"Call 911!" I yelled up the stairs. "Now!"

When I knelt beside her, I slipped my hand beneath her head to check for blood. No blood. I slipped gently behind her, stroking her forehead as I would do for Davis in a seizure.

"Stupid," she whispered. "Not tonight. Oh, I'm so dumb." She whimpered, "Why did I ruin Christmas?"

"Mom. This is not about a dinner or a day. We can do both any other time. Right now, let's be about you." I encouraged her to remember her breath, and she knew how to settle from her meditative practice. My sister Marcia brought down a headset and DVD player, which had my meditation music as we waited for the ambulance. Mom lay on the cold concrete floor and listened to the music as a few tears rolled down her cheek.

"I don't want an ambulance," she said.

"Mom." My hand stroked her pale cheek, too pale. "We're in this now. Stay with the music. I love you." My dad stood on the stairs she had fallen down, forlorn and helpless.

Falls happened to children like Davis, to parents like me, and to the elderly like my mom and dad. A slip could disrupt life plans as quickly as Davis's DNA had.

A paramedic appeared by my side to take control of Mom's head. They loaded her on a backboard and prepared her for transport. I answered their questions, and then I grabbed a bag with a few items in it for her because I felt she would not be coming home soon. I jumped in the ambulance. My sister, brother, and father followed in their car.

It was odd; they stood back, they deferred to my lead as if I had any more to say than they could. I didn't. It was just a habit to move her forward as quickly as possible into better hands because of my time learning to do this alongside Davis.

Once in the ER, my mother rated her pain as a one. I explained to the doctor the scale of pain tolerance by which my mother measures her many ailments. She did not want to be a bother or a burden to others around her. Mom was admitted to the hospital after spending the evening in the ER with seven rib fractures. While waiting for her to transfer to a hospital room from the ER, my siblings and I gathered with my father around the vending machine for our Christmas Eve dinner. I chose nuts.

Within a few days, the care and commitment required to mend after her stay in the hospital became obvious. But Mom had a fear of care centers. She pleaded with me to let her stay in our home. Of course, I agreed. She needed me. If I could Do Davis during these weeks at home on school break, I felt sure I could help my mother as well. I also had to help my father, who was not quite as sharp as his wife lay in a hospital bed away from him. I hoped having her near would help him as well.

I arranged for a hospital bed to be set up in my home, and we scheduled home nursing visits. My siblings departed, and our children stepped in to help. Ryan gently guided Mom up the stairs when we brought her home. We set a walker next to her bed so that we could help her use the bathroom every two hours. I wrapped a cowbell, from Ryan's ski racing days, to the railing so she could call for us when she needed help. Lynnell sat nearby, enjoying her grandparents' company for a longer period than a few days. We fed Mom soup and sat with her. When she asked for lamb, I knew she was getting a bit of her feistiness back. I managed the medication requirements for Davis, Mom, and Dad, only once stopping short of a mix-up before I nearly handed Mom's pain pill to Davis.

My dad's mental acuity, or lack thereof, slipped farther away as the stress of his new reality set in. He longed for his home and his wife beside him at night. His hearing aid was broken, so he smiled a lot when we asked him questions. I sent the hearing aid off to be repaired, and in the meantime, we all tried to speak up. The loud voices made Davis nervous, so he shied away from the chaos, sticking to his corner with the television.

Despite all of this, we did our best to keep dinner plans and follow our normal routines. We were preparing for a few dinner guests as Dad's television show blared over the noise of the house. Lucy, our dog, was barking. She also was in heat and wearing one of Davis's diapers with a hole snipped out for her tail. Davis was watching his TV, and I couldn't tell his program's sound from dad's. Both were loud. Rick was busy at the stove preparing part of the dinner. Then mom's nurse showed up. Nurse Ellen introduced herself as I led her up the stairs to mom's room. Davis promptly grabbed her hand to get her to help him change his television show to a new one. Just typical chaos, I thought.

I listened in as the nurse examined mom. Her blood pressure was too high, her oxygen saturation levels too low. The nurse called Mom's physician and declared that mom was not in a good situation. She needed to do more than to lay in her bed, and she needed 24/7 hands-on help as she healed. She needed occupational and physical therapy. I had hired someone to be with her at night, but that was not enough. They wanted her to be in a rehabilitation program to learn how to manage herself and her new, hopefully temporary, limitations.

The physician spoke to Rick. The odds were stacked against mom because of her seven rib fractures. The first three months of care were critical. I, the one who could manage Davis, had to finally admit I could not fully care for both my mother and my son. I felt that I had failed my mother, that I was not able to do for her what I had been doing for my son since he was born. We made arrangements to look at the place the hospital recommended nearby in Bishop for temporary healing.

Nurse Ellen came by to visit before mom left in an ambulance for the care center. She asked about the dog.

"Is she incontinent?"

I smiled.

"Just in heat," I replied. Then I tried to explain my world and our change in plans for Mom. Nurse Ellen was relieved that Mom would be moved elsewhere. I admitted that I felt that I had failed.

"I find you remarkable," she said.

Her kind words soothed and cloaked me like a warm blanket. I turned my attention to Davis and the odor that wafted from his diaper. "Duty calls," I said as I led him off to his room for a diaper change. "And thank you!"

I wanted to do more, be more for the others who asked for my help, but I accepted that Davis needed me most. He needed me to be healthy, not over-committed, and happy so that he could reflect back to me my smile and I, his. To achieve this, we needed more than just Guillermina. How much more help we would need, we did not yet know.

22

DIALOGUE WITH THE DIVINE

"Perhaps it is a good thing to have a beautiful mind, but
an even greater thing is to discover a beautiful heart."

John Nash

2011

The summer of 2011 felt full. Busy. We hiked and biked, and we
were a regular spectacle when Davis pedaled his adult-sized trike
since Rick and I would run behind him with a rope to act as his
brakes. We feasted on our son's good health. Our eldest, Ryan,
returned to Mammoth with his fiancé Sarah and married beneath a
tent in a meadow filled with friends and family. Our daughter flew in
from the East Coast to join in the celebration. Sarah kindly invited
Lynnell and Davis to be part of her lineup of groomsmen and bridesmaids. One of Ryan's groomsmen, a childhood friend, was in charge
of keeping Davis settled by rubbing his fingers through Davis's hair
as they stood beside Ryan. I appreciated that we could include Davis,
if only for a short time, because the community knew Davis and
our family. No explanation was needed. Ryan had two mother-son
dances, one with his mother and one with me. I felt pretty lucky in
August. But luck was its own trickster two weeks earlier.

I heard a long groan broken by gasps from his downstairs bedroom in the moments past midnight. Fear gripped my heart while
my mind clicked into action. I threw on my robe and flew down

the stairs to Davis's room. I saw my son beneath his summer comforter with his back arched, his limbs straight, his eyes open but disconnected.

"Come on, baby, mommy's here," I said to him as I settled in next to him. *God, why must you torture this child?* I tensed up, wishing to pull Davis back from wherever these seizures took him, to have him smile again, to ask him to toss a ball in my direction. I wanted this to be over. *Can it please be over?*

True to his pattern, the seizure ended after a minute. Davis slowly found his way back, his body melting onto his sheets, his mind dazed. Finally, after long, stretched moments, his eyes met mine. He was not yet able to focus, his lips lifted in a piece of a smile, not his former broad grin, but enough. It was enough for me.

"Oh baby, so sorry you have to go through all this," I hugged him and felt him snuggle against me. The pathos of the moment weighed heavy—my gratitude and relief for the end of another seizure pressed up against the reality that each episode stole a piece of his capacity, of his being, and of our child.

Afterward, the house was silent as Davis slept, but I was awake with my senses on high alert.

A second seizure came and went, and then Davis slept.

The adrenaline continued to push me. Davis rested. I could not. I was done for the night. It was three in the morning. I fluffed up a few pillows and nestled in beside my boy. Truthfully, he wasn't a boy anymore. Soon he would be sixteen.

And he would never drive a car.

Davis would never do many things, but that night I felt sad about this one milestone missed, for driving had meant so much to his older siblings. Earning their driver's license and their independence was a rite of passage for teenagers. Yet Davis would never drive a car or gain such freedom, and it broke my heart to acknowledge another milestone missed forever.

Davis snored heavily beside me with the fatigued sound that often followed a hard seizure. The wind gently brushed against the window, making a noise that kept Lucy, our dog, alert in the corner of the room.

I circled in on this sadness periodically, mixed in with the denial, anger, and bargaining which all accompany great loss. The sequence began early in the days of Doing Davis before fully knowing what that meant. The cycle seemed to circle back on itself over the years, with one phase dominating at any given time. At odd moments that darn sadness could sneak up on me. I wondered what he might have been like without his deletion. When I saw another child the same age as Davis laughing and engaging with their peers, meeting their milestones, and making plans for the future, I felt sorry for his losses. These thoughts choked me.

Back in college, I had the opportunity to take a class completely devoted to Elisabeth Kubler-Ross's five stages of grief and the process of coming to terms with death. The cycle was about moving toward acceptance in the face of loss because life is a series of gains and losses.

Over the years, I have referred back to this outline as guidance when I was stuck in the cycle, as I often was because I had planned life one way, and it snuck in with a different version. I used to pretend that it was okay, good 'ole denial. It always led the charge.

It was now five o'clock in the morning.

Davis was seizing again.

Rick appeared in the doorway, alert to the soft groan escaping from Davis as he disappeared in his electric brain storm. At least one of us caught some sleep. I predicted a long day ahead.

"Time for valium," I said.

Rick retrieved the rectal valium medication, and we administered the liquid via syringe after pulling down Davis's diapers. Within thirty minutes, Davis seized again, quickly moving from a frozen state to a prolonged series of spasms.

"Time for the ER?" Rick asked.

I nodded.

"I'll make some coffee and get the car ready."

I prepared a backpack of essentials, and then it was time to get Davis dressed. I slowly helped him up from the bed.

"Davis?" I panicked.

He was standing, reaching for me, but could not see me. His eyes were open, but they wandered. Instead, he held out his hand, and I locked mine onto his.

"Rick," I yelled out. "Hurry."

Rick was immediately beside me.

"His eyes. Look at his eyes."

Davis could not see.

"911," Rick called back to me as he left the room, visibly alarmed.

My mind and heart raced. *Will he be blind?*

Within minutes of Rick's 911 call, four paramedics arrived at the house. They paused before entering Davis's bedroom. Their eyes seemed to span the room, assess the space, identify their patient, Davis, on the bed beneath the quilt. Their eyes also rested on me, as I was wrapped around him like a shield.

I uttered, "He. Can't. See."

I remained silent after that, pressed back into the role of observer as they opened their bags and began their process.

The routine was god-awful familiar.

Three of the paramedics knew our family well, but the fourth was new. "Four" held a clipboard and scanned the room. His eyes lingered on the bear paw quilt I made that hangs above the bed and then on the oxygen compressor next to the bed. Four was middle-aged, not fit. Probably not a hiker or skier.

My breathing settled as I focused on something apart from Davis's new dilemma. I picked people and created narratives for someone I did not know, like Four, to pull myself up and away from my frightened heart when I needed to. I decided he fished.

Davis moaned. I stroked his leg, "I know, baby." He turned his face toward my voice, prompting his brown hair to drop onto his forehead. I swept back his hair, and my fingers brushed against one of his forehead scars.

This one came from smashing into a door jamb when he was five and still wobbly on legs not strong enough and not coordinated enough to keep up with the rest of his body. He loved to dive into the clothes dryer and pull out the warm bundles within. Some bundles were too heavy for him, and he would topple back, drop the bundle, and pop back into the dryer for more. In his unsteady gait, he had rushed toward me with an armful of warm clothes and crashed his head into the door jam. Blood flowed everywhere. Later, this same scar landed Rick with Davis in the ER when it burst because Davis had been banging his head while I was away at a writer's conference dinner.

Each mark had its own story. Another was from pulling a bar stool down on himself. Lynnell had quickly asked, "Is it my fault mommy?" "No," I replied. "He just toppled." Off we would go to the emergency room, Lynnell silently pressed up against a wall. Me, her mom, too focused on Davis to realize how many ER trips she followed us on. Yet another set of stitches for reaching out and missing the hand he sought on the stairs. He was small enough to roll without more damage than a cut near his mouth.

As I touched his pale skin, I noticed that his face was still moist from the sweat of the recent seizures. Convulsing was such hard work. To have them, to watch them unfold.

"When?" Four asked.

"When what?" I replied.

"When did you notice that he could not see?"

"Oh." I looked up.

I wanted to explain that this was my fault, the seizures, the lost sight, the ambulance. Mine. I felt responsible. I missed a cue, an opportunity to make it better. Somehow, I could have stopped this. I believed that I could. When did I notice that my son was blind?

"After the fourth seizure," my voice was calm, but my heart was shaking. Deep breath, "I did the rectal valium, but it did nothing to stop the momentum of the next seizure."

Four rushed his pen across the page as he tried to keep up with what I said. "After the fourth seizure, we knew it was time for the emergency room."

"I see," Four said. He was detached from us, engaged with paperwork. His upper lip looked sweaty.

The female paramedic I often saw around town stepped to the bed. She greeted Davis by name in the grocery store and did so again that morning. Davis turned his head toward her voice. I appreciated that she engaged him with words, though he could not reply.

Davis was a teenager, but his mind remained like that of a toddler's. He would never be left unattended. He would never reply with words. He could communicate with his eyes, or a Happy Dance, or tears. Basic emotions. He lacked the capacity for guile, for ego. When he found it in others, he veered away as if he sensed anger and discontent in one's soul. Again, he reminded us, as he had long ago, that as our gatekeeper he was attuned to the goodness of others' souls.

Outside the window, I heard the mountain chickadee with its sweet, easily recognizable song, which to me sounds like "cheeseburger." Davis loved cheeseburgers. I loved birdsong.

Four continued with the questions, "What is his condition?"

One of the paramedics looked toward me and nodded; he knew. He had done this paperwork before. The female paramedic prepared an IV, and I picked up the scent of rubbing alcohol. Davis whimpered. He knew the smell often came with a needle. "It's okay, sweetie," I said as I prepared to hold him if he flinched from the needle.

Rick appeared in the doorway. The slump of his shoulders looked so familiar, the posture of a parent who fears for the wellbeing of his child. Rick wanted to fix our world but couldn't. He met my gaze before speaking.

"It's a rare condition," Rick told Four, picking up where I left off. He explained that Davis was born with a deletion on the twenty-second chromosome, a condition recently named the Phelan-McDermid Syndrome. "He is the thirty-fourth to be diagnosed," Rick continued.

"In the state?" Four asked.

"In the world," we said, together.

I smiled at this togetherness, this unity created by Doing Davis. It took but a glance from one of us to the other, and we understood. *Need a diaper. Can you comfort him while I get his food ready? I need a hug.* The last one was usually from me.

My friend Deena once shared what she observed of our style after watching us host a roomful of guests in our home. Amidst the chatter, the music, and the replenishing of food and beverages for our guests, it was the look that Rick and I gave one another across the room that she saw. Of course, she notices bird behavior at the back end of a twenty-mile run—when most might be staring at the pavement—but she caught how Rick's eyes asked if I had given Davis his seizure meds due at that time, or should he? My eyes confirmed that the meds had been given and all was well.

I learned more about our approach to a complicated life circumstance through what Deena and other friends and family members told us that they saw. For us, we just did what needed to be done—as a team. If I pulled out eggs, Rick was holding a pan. If Davis convulsed, Rick had a stopwatch. If I was exhausted after our most recent medical crisis, Rick would settle me onto the couch for a day of retreat. We could finish each other's sentences and hold each other's dreams.

Four appeared to be overwhelmed by the rarity of our son's diagnosis. Me too. Especially when I had to explain it. My exclamation mark was always a big sigh. Four broke the lead on his pencil. I understood why. Our boy was new to him. He probably saw a young man in diapers making sounds no one could understand.

But he was missing the bigger scene: who our boy was. How Davis began our day by clapping before we guided him into his routines. He squealed with joy when the yellow school bus rounded the corner to our cul-de-sac. Sometimes he broke into his Happy Dance. No one could duplicate his stiff-legged hop from one foot to the other, though we had all tried. He ran and walked awkwardly as if permanently locked into heavy ski boots, but he was agile and full of delight when he danced.

Davis lacked words, but his squawks, staccato muttering, and tone did communicate: a high voice was joy, a low tone was a complaint. His abrupt sounds took some getting used to and startled those who didn't know him. Yet he always beckoned us into his world with his eyes, into his infectious play. Toss a ball his way and the games began. He could catch and throw well, but sometimes he deliberately aimed to the left to see us scamper sideways. He was mischievous and unpredictable, and for this he needed his vision. *Please?*

"Ready," announced one of the paramedics who had just brought in the chair for transport down the staircase.

I prayed.

Please, dear God, do not let Davis be blind.

I can do hospitals and late nights in an emergency room. I can even keep my son alive through the fiery hell of his seizures, but I cannot do blind. Not for Davis, it's just not fair to him. His world is already so small. Please let him see, and let us have this one small thing in common: to see our day and the beauty it holds, filled with people we love. Please?

As the paramedics prepared him for transport, I felt us all slipping down the rabbit hole of Davis's disability together once again, unsure of what lay ahead.

I realized that I had on my pajamas beneath my shirt. I ran upstairs to change into sweatpants and a warmer top layer. Hospitals felt so cold. I caught up with the paramedics as they made their way down the stairs from the second level to the street level with my son strapped into a chair and ever so frightened.

One of the team looked up at the art on the wall of the staircase; a series of oil paintings I did that I called "Mom." The first scene was of a mother bear gently nudging her cub. In the background stood the famous face of El Capitan in Yosemite. The next canvas was an African scene with a cub's arm playfully placed over the shoulders of his parent, a lioness, as she stared off toward the dry plains. The third painting depicted an alert doe watching out while her fawn rested in a cluster of aspens. In the next painting, a dolphin protected her young near a bed of kelp and rock. Next to this canvas were penguins, and here I showed as many as I could, with one in particular holding her egg on her feet. The last canvas was my favorite: an elephant, weary, face etched in lines of fatigue, gazing across a river at her source of food. She could not yet cross the rapid river because her young one was too small to navigate the currents. The baby needed time to develop more strength. As the mother waited, the herd would wait too. This was the message I clung to and how I had been raised. We would stand beside our feeble, those not strong enough to cross. We would make that walk forward together.

The paramedic looked back toward me. They had just passed the elephant canvas at the bottom of the steps. I was still at the top of the stairs, fearfully holding my breath. Seeing Davis on the stairs, even in transport, always scared me. When they reached the bottom of the stairs safely, I released my breath with relief.

I ran through the living room to grab a few Jimmy Neutron and SpongeBob DVDs for Davis. Finally, I added diapers and extra clothes for Davis to the backpack before following the team out to the ambulance. Rick was beside Davis. *Bless him for this*, I thought, *always beside his son*. I climbed into the ambulance and sat on the metal bench beside the gurney. I knew this position well; I was not in the way of the paramedics but still close to my son. Rick headed for the car and would follow the ambulance. This, too, was part of our routine.

"Davis, Mom is here," I told him, and he turned toward my voice. My hand tousled his hair, and he leaned into the feel of my fingers. I wanted to cry. It was so sad to see him like this.

Once we were all at the hospital, Rick and I settled into the emergency room with Davis for the next four hours. Medications administered through an IV finally stopped the seizures. The plan was to observe and see if the seizure cycle was over. Rick worked on a file for one of his cases while fielding intermittent calls from his office. I was sketching Davis as he slept.

After the seizures stopped, Davis's vision returned. A neurologist suggested that the seizures had temporarily disrupted the brain's pathways. I gladly accepted this. I would accept anything that might negate the need for further testing.

Once we were released from the hospital, we made our way back home in silence, feeling shaken yet relieved. Rick and I assisted Davis up the stairs and into his bed, where he slept on and off. The seizures did not return. We said little as we prepared dinner. Later, Rick and I made our way up the stairs to our bedroom. I adjusted the baby monitor for sound. We all slept without interruption.

The next morning, after Rick left for his office, I began to feel angry and unsettled about our close call with blindness the day before. Between Rick's departure and the arrival of our son's favorite caretaker, Guillermina, I paced. I arranged Davis in his chair, a large double-wide chaise lounge in the living room, and I paced some more. My angst continued to build.

The doorbell rang, and Davis's "other mom" arrived and came upstairs to kiss her boy. I felt some solace and smiled because so many people loved my son. He brought good hearts into our home.

"Thank you, Guillermina," I said.

"Oh, he is my boy. You go now, I have him. We are good," she assured me. She was a woman born to be a mom. I was still trying to figure out when to lead and when to watch with all of our children. "He is fine. I pray for him, and I know he is good now. God tells me this."

I quickly left because I was furious at God, at fate. My beliefs were complicated because I grew up in the church, but I had explored eastern philosophies. Throughout my life, I had felt guided and supported by what I could only call synchronicity. I had come up with a strong belief that the beauty in the world and the challenges in our experiences have a source, a benevolent source. A Sufi prayer that I learned from my parents when they began to practice Sufism alongside their Christian faith expressed it best for me:

Toward the One
the Perfection of Love, Harmony, and Beauty
the Only Being
United with all the Illuminated Souls
Who form the Embodiment of the Master,
the Spirit of Guidance.

To quell my mounting anger, I drove a mile away to a trailhead and set off on a path I had taken many times. With so many trails surrounding our area, it was not hard to be alone. Once alone, I unleashed my emotions.

I shook my right fist in the air and yelled at the source of life, "Why Davis?"

Angry tears streamed down my cheeks and chilled my face in the cool morning breeze.

"Pick on me! Not him."

My feet strode evenly across the bumps of the mountain trail while my voice and emotions tripped me up. I yelled and sobbed into the thin, quiet air where there was no one to hear my anguish. I ran deeper into the mountains, looking for a place of peace to hold me during this turbulent fit of frustration.

Why does this little cherub suffer so much?

My feet struck the path harder and harder, and my thighs felt the impact, then my hips. Pain. I slowed down and calmed my breath. I looked around and noticed that the meadow path curved toward the trees. Water sloshed across the rocks and ruffled the sand of a shallow streambed bedside the path. My thoughts absorbed the world around me. The topmost branches of the pines swept the blue sky while the lower limbs hugged the ground. Aspens clustered near more water a few hundred yards away.

A deer broke through the brush ahead and shook leaves loose from the branches as she moved. The graceful animal landed near the path's edge. For a moment, our eyes met, a split second before the deer skittered off toward the grove of aspens. I held the image of the doe's eyes locked onto mine. Like Davis, her gaze contained a simple *knowing*—pure inner peace, pure innocence.

I settled. It was over. I would be fine. My legs continued their run. I felt the air inside my mouth and nose sliding down my throat, expanding and releasing in my chest with each deep breath. More tears flowed, but these salty trickles soothed me. I was grateful that Davis had survived so much. That we all had.

Ahead of me was a campground. I smelled the smoke of the morning campfires. Near a tent, a family rattled metal pans as they prepared to cook. Their children warmed themselves beside the small fire. A bundled-up man offered a woman a steaming mug. My heart warmed.

I remembered such moments of rustic pleasures camping with my own family when the children were younger, and I longed for that familiar comfort. The campers made being a family look so simple and easy.

I turned back toward the start of my run. My soul, untethered and free from my petulant mood, guided us home. I rubbed my temples, no longer troubled by what I decided were my own seizures of the heart.

2011 Greetings from the Mammoth Woods!

Since we haven't written a letter in several years, we will compress about three years' worth of "highlights" into this year's effort. First, however, we trust that all of you who receive this letter are happy and well. We hope that you will have a happy and prosperous 2012.

As our children move forward with their own lives, Cheryl and I can't help but think about how fortunate they (and we) have been to experience our mountain paradise for nearly twenty years now. There is a certain grounding effect of these mountains and a sense of community which we continue to cherish. Despite last season's snowfall of fifty-six feet, we still love it here!

Our youngest, Davis, is now sixteen and is enrolled at Mammoth High School in a special education program. He continues to have his share of medical setbacks as a result of a seizure disorder, but his conviction and courage pull him through each crisis. He has become an iconic figure in Mammoth and is always happy. (Why would he not be—he is surrounded by women all day who love him to death!) He continues to enjoy skiing in the winter and boating in the summer.

Lynnell just turned twenty-two and has been enrolled at Smith College in Massachusetts. The 3,000-mile distance between us makes it difficult for Cheryl and me to see her as often as we would like to. She is able to take classes at four other colleges in the area, including Amherst College and UMass. The east coast presents a different culture from that of California, but she has adapted. In between school terms, she has managed to experience several different types of low-paying entry-level jobs, which has shown her why a college education is so important!

Ryan has experienced an extraordinary last three years. He graduated from Chapman University Law School in May, took the California bar exam in July, moved back to Mammoth and married a Mammoth local, Sarah Butner, in August, joined my law firm in September, passed the bar exam in November, and has become an associate attorney working for me. He is the first-ever to graduate from Mammoth High and return as a practicing attorney. He also continues to race-coach part-time at

Mammoth Mountain. As you can imagine, Cheryl and I are thrilled to have two of our three children home in Mammoth. I am particularly happy because his joining my firm coincides with the beginning of my plan to begin to work less and play more. (So far, it is just an attempt!)

Cheryl has spent the last three years managing the affairs of the Wood tribe and recovering from two shoulder surgeries. All of those years of downward dog yoga have finally caught up to her! She and I get over to our place in Maui regularly, usually with Davis, who loves the environment there. Cheryl has become a prolific artist: quilting, painting, and ceramics. She has enthusiastically enrolled in several art and art history classes at the community college, which she finds time to participate in while caring for Davis and working part-time as an administrator in my office.

I have been recovering from surgeries as well following a hip cartilage tear at the Boston Marathon in 2009. I have resumed distance running, and at age sixty achieved a personal record at the San Jose half marathon in October. I am looking forward to my first post-injury marathon in Houston in January 2012 and am planning on setting a new personal record there as well. Here is to health! In 2010, I returned to public service by running for and winning a seat on the Mammoth Lakes Town Council. So, we are in the thick of it.

The Woods

23

PLANS?

"May your choices reflect your hopes, not your fears."

Nelson Mandela

2012

From the time he could crawl, Davis always had two favorite places to be—by a beach or in a lake. As a toddler he would leapfrog in a gentle ocean shore break. Dressed in a life vest, he bobbed around with us in the ocean and lakes. Davis would scramble off the back end of our boat to float in the lake, and sometimes he would take an inner tube ride with me as Rick and the other children sat in the boat cheering Davis on. He loved the attention. Later, when the older children moved on in their own lives, we added a paddleboard to the boat and slowed our boat pace down. Davis liked speed, but Rick and I became a bit more cautious once it was just the three of us.

During our vacations to the beach, Davis had a game on shore that required tremendous patience for those who participated. It was Ryan who taught us all the game of surrendering to Davis by the shore years ago. Davis had a cast on his left arm, which he broke in a fall from a seizure at school. He could not go in the water. Ryan held his hand, followed him this way and that, and Davis loved taking the lead. No water, only sand. Back up to his parents, back down to the shore break in Del Mar. Simply watching the two of them relaxed my mind and settled something within me. There was no agenda, just camaraderie. Being present to a gentle young boy. The next time

Rick and I had Davis by the water, we too surrendered. This game was a gift and we willingly played along. Near the sea, sometimes he would put in a toe, then more of his leg, and finally, if I went ahead of him, he would get into the water to float and catch me. Then we would all play "pop-up" in the water together. Rick or I would go under the water and pop up. *Wheee!* He would clap.

We were by the water in Maui with Davis and our friends Ed and Mary playing these games with our son who was getting bigger and bigger. This felt normal for us. Rick and I never thought much about what our games looked like to others. Apparently, Ed had concerns.

At dinner later that night, he asked me one question, "What are your plans?"

Davis, sixteen, was with a babysitter.

"Your long-term plans for Davis?" he clarified.

"Ed," I replied to him, "to say thank you at the end of the day for three things." I smiled, content to be done with this topic. Davis and his good health were always part of my thank you to the stars above after the panic I had felt about Davis losing his sight.

"You can't stop me on this Cheryl. I can see it taking a toll on you both, but especially on you. You need a plan."

I looked toward Rick for a rescue, but he was engaged in a conversation with Mary, who knew more about Davis's mounting health issues these past years. I had made the mistake of wondering aloud how long I could physically Do Davis on a call once with Mary. I had been at a low point when fatigue wore me down.

"I hear you, Ed. I do."

I refused to discuss the issue any further, though I knew that eventually I would need to address Davis's future. Davis was my size and I worked out hard just to keep fit enough to handle him.

Let me use Scarlett's "Gone with the Wind" line and "think about that tomorrow, on our long trek home," I thought. *Not now.*

The next day we managed to get through airport security with Davis in a wheelchair and our service dog Lucy alongside him. Two years earlier I had completed a program to train her for service. To do so, I had driven her down to my parents' home in Oceanside every other week. This had allowed me to keep up on my parent's changing situation as they aged and to have a break from caretaking Davis. We had hired help to come into our home after he came home from school and on weekends, which made a tremendous difference for me and my psyche.

To get through TSA, I removed Lucy's leash and collar and commanded her to go forward and sit. I sent my shoes, bags, and other belongings through the scanner, after which I retrieved Lucy and collared her up.

Davis took a bit more time. We always had him in a wheelchair in crowded spaces for his comfort, but security had to scan the chair for dangerous substances without him in it. Davis complained because they had his chair. He was then patted down before he could return to his seat. Lucy took up her position beside him and off we went.

I had to remind Rick how he hated to be a spectacle, "Just look at us now honey." He had mellowed, surrendered I supposed. Davis forced us into a slower pace when he was not in a medical crisis.

We parked Davis in his chair, and Lucy beside him, near a wall by the gate for departure back to California. A kindly older lady came over to us. She reached out for Davis's hand, which he eagerly gave her.

"Hello," she said. Davis wiggled and shifted about in his chair which was his signal that he wanted to get that chair in motion.

"What's your name?" the woman asked.

He stared, content not to complain for the moment.

"He can't speak," I explained. "But thank you for saying hello to him."

I held out my hand to meet hers. She did not let my hand go for a moment. I felt as if a long-lost companion had found us. Was it her compassion that was so familiar? Her patience? She seemed completely at ease with Davis's behavior, as difficult as he was at the moment.

"I had a son, like him, with cerebral palsy," she shared, her eyes misting a bit. My tear ducts copied hers. Sharing scars on the heart from one mom to another always seemed to cause the eyes to flood. "He died."

"Oh," I said, "I'm sorry for your loss." An awkward moment passed as she continued to smile at Davis. "How old was he when he passed?" I asked.

"Sixty-one."

Sixty-one!

I was fifty-four. Davis was almost seventeen. How old could she be?

"I lost Skipper and my husband within two years of each other. Miss them." Her expression shifted, back to a warm smile. "But I'm remarried, and I just had to say hello to your boy. What's his name?"

"Davis."

Her new husband walked over to retrieve his wife so that they could catch an earlier flight. I wanted to ask her so much more, like *How?* I viewed her as yet another ally ahead of me on this journey. I felt grateful for the brief encounter.

For Davis, the flight home was as awful as the flight over, but my attitude had shifted. Over the past few years, Davis had developed a difficult new trait best summed up as Obsessive-Compulsive Disorder (OCD). At school he needed to close drawers and doors. Soon that obsession came home as well, and we often removed our hands from a drawer just in time not to have it crushed. His obsession was about things that he knew could close. He wanted them closed. As we sat in the airplane, he watched someone close an overhead bin. He popped up to close the rest. Rick and I had to lay across Davis to contain him. Finally, I gave him one of his valium pills, used for such a moment to calm him down.

Sixty-one?

I reminded myself I could do this, one day at a time, just as I, as we, always had. Perhaps that was enough of a plan until circumstances required a revision. I thought it was a good plan.

24

AGING UP AND THROTTLING BACK

"For it's our grief that gives us our gratitude…"

Amanda Gorman, *The Miracle of Morning*

2013

The blunt, rounded end of the left stern cleat, designed to wind rope around, not skin, punched into the back of my right thigh as I slammed down hard on the edge of the boat. I still had Davis in a lock-handed grip as I swung his head away from the outboard motor and motionless propeller.

A simple mishap occurred as I loaded an eighteen-year-old, 125-pound adult child with special needs onto the boat after a swim in the lake. An easy moment shifted to disaster.

I tried to release Davis, clad in his life vest, safely back into the water, but Davis did not release my hands.

I was held back, my thigh stuck on the cleat, and, at the same time, pulled by Davis overboard. I felt and saw my leg tear open, and in my mind, I saw a chunk of my back right thigh flapping open in the water as I sank into the lake. When I popped up, I saw the white of the boat and the murk of the lake. I realized that I was intact, some-what, and had to get back to the boat as soon as possible. I convinced myself, still mindful and not yet in terror, to pull myself up to the surface. My mind began to register panic as the pain came on from the wound in my leg. I hoisted myself onto the back platform of the boat and yelled to Rick, who was on shore thirty feet away. I stepped my working leg, the left leg, onto the swim ladder before hoisting myself onto the back of the boat.

It felt okay to panic now, but Rick did this aloud for us both

"Oh Cheryl, oh my god," Rick yelled from shore. "Oh my god!"

Like any mishap, this one was quick, the aftermath slow, painfully slow.

Every summer, our family boat-camped at Lake Don Pedro near Yosemite National Park. We drove three hours, from door to dock, through the park and surrounding mountains. We had made this trek every year, sometimes multiple treks when our schedules allowed. The older kids no longer joined us, but sometimes friends did. The water remained warm in late summer, and the campsite we liked was nice and shady and away from the other sites. Sometimes we water skied, sometimes we just floated and swam. Davis always wore a life vest, as did our dog Lucy, who liked to tube with us behind the boat, her brown ears flapping in the wind and causing other boaters to hoot or blow their horn when we passed them. Davis clapped; he loved boating, loved the wind, and loved when Rick made a big splash after a fall or when he dove in. Life on the water seemed easy, slow, and one of the few things we could actively do with Davis.

This trip was no different at first. We had set up camp and settled down for the night—only for our sleep to be rudely interrupted by a midnight group yelling to one another as they set up their camp. We were not the only campers to be woken up. Soon we heard voices yelling at them to be quiet, and the noisy campers invited the voices to, "Shut up yourselves!"

We woke to the kinder sounds of birds and other campsites stirring. Soft voices, the clanking of pots on the portable stoves, coffee. I loved coffee at the campsite. Rick was always up early, and when I popped out of the tent that morning, he handed me a steaming mug with just enough milk and sugar to make the drink lethal. Davis bellowed his approval of dawn before we asked him to quiet down

Other campers nearby started their sunrise serenade, but much louder than we usually hear on other trips. Engines revved up, campers yelled loudly to one another, and Davis resumed his morning vocalizations. The midnight madness group eventually emerged, having had the fewest hours of sleep, and I swear I saw every other camper near their site smiling. "Luck of the draw" we called it when we had noisy camp neighbors. Vengeance came from those whose sleep had been interrupted by the midnight marauders.

That morning we loaded Davis into the boat at the campsite rather than at the dock because we could be quite a spectacle when we hoisted and turned him onto the back deck in front of the other boaters. It required two of us to maneuver Davis up and onto the boat. We snapped on his life jacket and put one on the dog. Rick towed us down the ramp, launched us, and off we went to play in the lake for the day. We headed down the channel to our special swimming spot in a no-wake zone. It was eleven o'clock. I dove in, and Davis scrambled down to chase me in the water and pulled me back towards the boat. Lucy circled us in her life vest or chased her ball when Davis threw it. Rick headed over to shore with Lucy to help her take care of her business before we took off to tube. It was a typical morning before the accident.

I sobbed as I sat in the boat waiting for Rick to return with Lucy. I wanted to rewind just those last few minutes, like a video, and to have made a different choice about bringing Davis aboard by myself.

Rick swam back to the boat from shore and hauled Davis into the boat. He approached me with a towel to wrap around the wound. He then fired up the engine to find a spot with better cell reception.

"911." He was not asking me; he was telling me. The plan was to call 911.

We drove to the middle of the lake. He told me not to look at my wound. So, of course, I did. I saw pieces of my leg fat on the towel and wanted to vomit.

Rick reached emergency services on the cell phone and made arrangements to meet at the dock. During all of this, Davis was quiet, watchful, and unusually still.

"Just breathe," Rick reminded me. Our family motto seemed to be "Just breathe."

We continued toward the gas dock, where two rangers waved us in. A ranger tied off our boat, and the paddleboard was removed from the deck. Lucy sat in the front open hull space to make room for more people to come on board. Davis stared at me. I cried as softly as I could because I did not want to frighten him. The rangers began asking me questions: My name, do I know where I am? How old am I?

"Fifty-five," I answered.

"Damn," said Ranger Two. "You look good for fifty-five!"

I could not help but laugh, and this made Davis smile. Ranger Two had purposefully diverted me from my panic, I thought. My mind settled.

The questions continued. Did I hit my head? They pulled out an oxygen canister but did not know how it worked. I reached over to show them what to attach and what to turn. They wanted a high flow, I didn't. Rick mentioned his concern about my fall into the lake, he thought I hit the boat and that my neck was swollen.

Ranger One reached for a neck brace to wrap around and stabilize my neck, which did not hurt. Ranger Two yelled, "Oh, forget about it. I'll just hold her neck!" He sat behind me, holding my head in place while we waited for the ambulance and paramedics to arrive—they had been waiting for us at another dock. Both Rick and I were smiling from the humorously chaotic presence of these two. It helped.

A fire truck arrived. Then the lake patrol pulled up. A crowd gathered around the boat, curious about all the fuss and commotion.

Someone taped my leg in an attempt to hold the flesh together. Then I began the painful process of getting off the boat. I shuffled to the edge of the boat and shifted myself onto the back deck on my left butt cheek. From there, I was hoisted onto a gurney. As they wheeled me away, I heard Rick yell.

"Wait!" he called after us. "Where are you taking my wife?"

"Sonora Regional Medical Center."

The paramedic who took charge of the boat scene wanted to administer morphine. I hated painkillers because I did not tolerate them well. I explained the nausea issue, and she administered an anti-nausea medicine through the IV. When did I get an IV? Then came the morphine.

It's cool. I can do this. Okay, let it drip.

The emergency room was over-filled with patients on gurneys spilling out into the hallway with medical personnel rushing about from one to the next. Once they assessed my situation, I was left in a room with two other patients, one with a potential heart attack and the other just moaning. On morphine, I happily dealt with questions about the accident, processed their information about the stitches my leg required inside and out, and, yes, I could get another blanket because I was still in my swimsuit.

The morphine blurred time. Rick appeared, and then we headed home with me floating on a final dose of morphine while laying in the back seat.

Later I learned that after the paramedics took me from the boat, Rick drove back to the boat launch ramp, reloaded the boat onto the trailer with Davis in the boat, then broke down our campsite with Davis in the car. Davis was unusually cooperative, as if sensing that his dad needed to do other tasks and not try to figure out what Davis's whine meant.

Once home, Rick re-dressed the wound on my back thigh. Friends stopped by and suggested we might not be doing as well as we thought we were and that we needed to rethink our role in Davis's life.

We, Rick and I, were not invincible.

We were aging.

Our special needs child was a lot to handle.

I hurt. I slept. Later, Rick and I discussed our options.

"I want to sell the boat," Rick stated.

I had already come to this conclusion. The minor mishap could have been so much worse. We could have lost Davis, and we still could if he fell in just the wrong way. He was no longer a child; he was now a young man.

Later the next day, my friend Deena came by and, in her wonderfully wise way, invited us to consider that while one chapter closed, meaning boating, another would be opening. We were not surrendering to having less of a life without boating, but rather opening up our options to do other things—like paddleboarding—safely, with Davis.

We envisioned a new chapter. One without a boat but that included water because Davis loved the water. We decided that we, the Woods, remained lucky. We also accepted that it was time for a plan, one where Davis would have support if anything happened to us. Luckily, this part was made easier because of our involvement in California's generous Self-Determination program.

The accident opened our eyes.

From Rick's perspective, it reopened a topic we had long avoided. Before the boat mishap, when local specialists who followed our son's health and disability had approached us about our plans for Davis's future, Rick's reaction had been defensive.

"What do you mean?" he had asked.

"Well, Davis will be eighteen in four months," the nurse had answered. "Have you made plans for him?"

Rick, who was mildly offended, had answered, "Don't worry, I will initiate conservatorship proceedings before he ages up." He was a lawyer, after all, he reminded me.

The nurse tried a different tact by gently yet directly stating what she had implied, "Where will he live, and with whom?"

Rick shot back, "Davis will live with us." End of discussion.

After the boat accident, we realized that a day would come when others would care for Davis. And we acknowledged that one day he would no longer live with us.

As Rick recalled:

> In 2013, it became clear that the "plan" had to include suitable housing for Davis outside of our home and to engage care providers who would love and care for him. Not unique, but a challenge nonetheless. First, a paradigm shift for me. Second, persuading Cheryl to go along with the plan. This took a while. But we made a plan. No, we embarked upon a mission for Davis's destiny, one which we could accomplish only with Self-Determination.

Unimaginable as it had seemed up until the accident, we needed a plan.

25

CRISIS, WHAT CRISIS?

"Fate is what happens to you. Destiny is how you respond."

Jim Curtan, *When You're Falling, Dive*

2014

The spring after our boating accident, a two-week interlude with Davis in Maui allowed us a much-needed break from a snowy winter in the Sierra. Davis had enjoyed a season of skiing with Disabled Sports Eastern Sierra, which strengthened him enough to walk more on this vacation than ever before. He enjoyed his walks along the boardwalk and around the neighborhood. We cherished this healthy version of our son.

After two weeks, we said goodbye to our favorite part of the ocean. We were always a bit wistful as West Maui disappeared in the rearview mirror and we left the islands.

We boarded our plane, and Davis settled in by the window. A flight attendant took plastic off the seat behind us as we stored our headphones and food for Davis. I pulled a piece of plastic off the seat in front of me. It was new, as in a brand new plane. The plane took off.

Just then, Davis began to seize.

"Seizure?" Rick asked as he leaned over to touch Davis.

I held Davis to protect his head from hitting the hard surfaces near the window and waited out the first part of the event where his back arched and his legs stiffened. Then he spasmed and shook. Once done, he slept. Rick had been aware of what was happening as he sat on the aisle seat and I sat in the middle next to Davis. His shoulders settled back, as did mine once our son slept away in his post-seizure fatigue.

An hour later, I felt Davis convulsing again. I pressed him into me as I stared through the plane window out toward the white clouds and blue sky.

The flight attendant came by with the refreshment cart just as Davis tumbled forward with his convulsion phase. She stared as I wrapped myself around Davis to keep him safe as his arms and legs flailed and twitched.

"He's seizing," the attendant told us, panic apparent in her voice.

"It's his second," Rick replied calmly as a parent who could do no more than watch his son in his seizure.

At this moment, we lost all control of the situation.

"Is there a doctor on the plane?" the flight attendant announced over the intercom.

Holy crap. That's for us!

Within moments, I spotted the attendant heading down the aisle toward us with someone close behind. He appeared to be uncomfortable. We certainly were.

"I'm a doctor," he shared. "They want me to assess the situation. Can you tell me what's going on?"

"Davis has a rare chromosome deletion," I began, and the doctor readily understood the explanation as I described how his condition manifested and where the seizures came in. "It's never happened on a plane before."

"You know I have to ask you this, but I can tell you have this down. You've been dealing with this for a while?"

"Yes."

"What's your plan?"

"I want to give him an extra Keppra pill now, crushed, but I don't have any apple sauce…"

The attendant near us called out, "Can anyone give us apple sauce here?"

I cannot tell you how many small containers of applesauce began to make their way toward us, passed off above the seats—a rather poetic moment, had it not been for the embarrassment. I opened one up and gave Davis his extra pill carefully, aware that it was yet another problem if he seized during this feeding.

"Okay, what happens if he has another one?" asked the doctor.

"I have Diazepam in my bag. I administer it rectally." However, I hoped not to, not here, on a plane. *Please be okay now, Davis.*

The attendant hung close by and patrolled our area like a hawk. Each time she passed, I smiled. Davis was sleeping again; his nose pressed up against the plastic fumes of the new plane.

Then, he seized.

Bad.

The attendant rushed forward and told everyone around us to take their seat immediately. Then she ran back to the intercom to announce this to all who did not hear her scream it. Rick had stepped out into the aisle to give me more room. I was not aware of the eyes upon us until Davis's body was still. Then I noticed the silence within the plane except for the roar of the engines.

Rick reached for the overhead bin and pulled out the Diazepam.

"What do you need?" barked the attendant.

Okay. Think. Breathe. What I needed was space; I could not walk this child down to the bathroom to administer the medicine.

"I have to lay him out, pull down his diapers and inject the medicine into his rectum." I paused. *How to do this? What do I need?* "Okay, I really don't want these kids around us to have their first frontal shot of a male here on a plane." By now, I counted five children under the age of eight leaning over their seats to watch us. "Any ideas?"

The attendant went to the back of the plane and made another announcement on the intercom. "All children in rows thirty through thirty-six need to go to the back of the plane with their parents now."

I hated this.

Really?

Does the whole plane have to know we have this happening here?

I laid Davis out across the three seats, and his legs dangled over. As I maneuvered his pants down to get to his diapers, I noticed blankets above us like curtains. Passengers and attendants held these up. The attendant we had been working with peeked out over her portion of the curtain. The task was tough, I tugged the pants down, then the diapers.

"Did you get it?" asked Rick from behind curtain number one.

"I'm trying to find the opening."

My fingers, as everyone around us now heard, probed for a rectal spot. Once found, I inserted the Diazepam syringe and squeezed slowly. I had only one shot at this. Literally.

Then, time to re-dress the boy—the man.

I tore the side of Davis's interior diaper to remove it because it was soaked with urine from the seizures; his bladder expunged more than an ordinary amount of pee. Two diapers remained. When we traveled, we always had multiple diapers on Davis, which made it easier to remove the inner one without undressing him. I pulled up the diapers and zipped up his pants. *Done. Whew!*

Davis met my gaze before he disappeared into a drugged stupor and slept. I headed down the aisle toward the bathroom to wash my hands. All eyes fell upon me. Mothers looked with kindness and children with curiosity. A few looked away.

As the plane taxied into the San Diego airport, we saw emergency vehicles with lights flashing and heard the whine of their sirens. Paramedics came down the aisle once the plane door opened, led by the attendant who handled our crisis. They wanted us off first. With a paramedic in front of Davis and one behind helping to hold him up, they moved forward. Davis was smiling, wobbly, and a bit confused by the new deplaning routine.

I followed the paramedics. Hands reached out to touch me.

Women said, "Bless you," and, "God has a plan."

Some said, "Take care."

Rick and I have heard these types of comments a lot, and we have never known quite how to reply except to say, "Thank you."

What they missed, as they seemed to pity our experience, were the fun parts that far outweighed the challenging ones. Rick—with his wicked sense of humor that always emerged in tough moments—had his own version of our departure from the plane. He recounted that as hands reached out to touch me and heads leaned out to watch me, he came up behind with our loose bags full of the food, meds, and toys for Davis.

"Pardon me. Excuse me. Could I get through here, please?" Rick had joked.

This made me laugh. We, the Woods, were a spectacle. Rick and I had misadventures like this so often that we turned them into stories that we shared with friends and family.

"Just another tale to tell," said Rick.

We placed Davis in his wheelchair as paramedics, firefighters, police, and airport personnel tried to convince us to transport Davis to the local hospital. Rick and I saw our son clap. Davis smiled. Crisis over. We knew, without need to explain to anyone else, that we had this one handled, and we wanted to take our son home, which we did.

"You hijacked the plane, pal," I told him with a smile.

Davis clapped again, oblivious to how much we all orbited around his condition. At the end of a crisis, there was always a sweet space to reflect on how lucky we were to land well. When someone asked me, "How do you do it," as people did, I often replied, "One hard moment with a sweet interlude on its tail at a time."

Davis had hijacked our lives, not just the plane. To admit this was not to whine about our circumstance but rather an observation about caretaking. It simply was. He kept life interesting and brought out the best in those around him.

26

THE SHARING OF TALES

"Tears are words that need to be written."

Paulo Coelho

2016

In the summer of 2016, Rick and I made it to the annual PMSF conference. It was our first in a few years. While we liked to attend all together with Davis, we had missed a few of the conferences when Davis's health was bad. This time around, we opted to have him remain home with care providers.

Whenever we attended these conferences, we reconnected with old friends on a familiar path with their childern and shared what we knew about the many medical issues of 22q. The topic of seizures had been introduced a few years before. In 2012, I was asked to give a presentation about seizures from a parent's perspective, along with another parent. At the 2016 conference, a neurologist made the presentation. Our group had come a long way in finding experts to volunteer their time and information. During the talk, I sat at a back table with Dr. Katy Phelan, who was always in attendance at the conferences. She was like our good sister, aunt, and mentor. I adored her sense of humor, and Rick and I shared time with her during these events.

My stomach lurched as the speaker moved forward in his presentation. Not enough data existed on older patients with seizures because many died of seizures. I recalled from earlier discussions about seizures that the patient could die from hitting a hard surface or having a seizure that would not break until the heart stopped. Even less data was available for older persons with PMS and seizures, like my son. I jumped up, left, and found the bathroom where I cried in one of the stalls. In between sobs, I heard another crying.

"Seizure presentation?" I asked with a voice still muffled by sobbing.

"Yes," I heard, between her sobbing.

I opened my stall door, and she opened hers. Out stepped one of the original parents I recognized from long ago. We hugged one another. We found two chairs in a seating area inside the bathroom. We sat together, and I listened to her story.

Her daughter had recently suffered her first seizure. When the ambulance arrived, the medics decided that drugs were involved because her daughter was an adult. The parents tried to explain that she was disabled. The medics would not listen and bound her daughter to the gurney. They did not allow the parents to be in the ambulance. In the ER, the parents were not allowed to attend to their child at first. Finally, the parents persuaded the staff that their daughter was not typical, did not do drugs, and was having her first seizure. By the time the mother could get to her child, her daughter was stripped down to her underwear, bound to a gurney, and terribly frightened. Her seizure had ended, but the experience was awful.

I cried with the other mother for the helplessness she and her daughter felt, for the ignorance of others, for the despair of that first seizure. We eventually left the bathroom, found our husbands, and talked about the need to educate more medical personnel about our children. Her husband had written a fifty-page introduction for parents new to the world of PMS. We felt that more still needed to be shared with the rest of the world.

The next topic discussed at the conference was placement—that difficult need to plan a child's care and housing as parents aged. Though we had discussed it, Rick and I were not yet ready to go down that path. Perhaps Rick was, but he deferred to me. Davis had rebounded that summer and was able to ride his bike again. He tossed balls and clapped. His Happy Dance had not resurfaced, but perhaps it would with time, I hoped.

On the second evening, we gathered with the parents we had met at the original PMSF conference back in 2000. We all felt like family. Sadly, we were missing a couple from Canada whose daughter was older than Davis. We had followed their lives as best we could and learned from them; they were the trailblazers. They had been ahead of us in tackling issues such as caretaking and placement back when we did not have help and refused to consider the option of Davis living apart from us.

That evening we laughed, and we shared the inside jokes of our unique reality with the other 22q parents. They enjoyed hearing Rick's funny stories about life alongside Davis. What I think they enjoyed most was that, as hard as our experiences had been, Rick and I still could laugh. We could separate from the drama once we passed through a crisis. Rick could take a simple event and make it a humorous, twenty-minute story. It was how we managed Doing Davis. By retelling our tales. And for me, by writing.

At the PMSF conference that summer, we also learned about a new drug trial in New York for seizure patients, and Davis qualified because he had PMS.

We signed on.

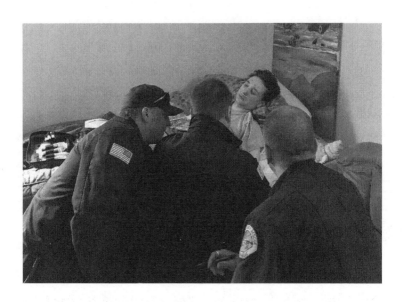

27

TAM OR HURKEY

"This being human is a guest house. Every morning a new arrival."

Jalal al-Din Rumi

2017

One Maui morning in January, I sipped my coffee on the lanai and stared west toward the ocean. Rick was out on his early run, and I had a book in hand as I waited for Davis to wake up. My favorite parts of the day in Maui were the early morning hours and sunset. The birds serenaded to greet the sun and to say goodbye. A plumeria tree by the back lanai provided a wonderful floral scent when in bloom and decorated the lawn with white flowers as they slipped from the branches. In winter, the tree was bare, but my nose remembered. An occasional whale spout could be spotted on the ocean horizon during whale season from December to March, as well.

Our son was now twenty-one. We mentally celebrated this milestone while anxiously awaiting for him to return to his former self. His health had been off these past few months. His balance was gone. He had skied only once this winter with DSES using a ski chair, operated mainly by an instructor. I saw concern on the faces of those who knew Davis from former healthy times, when his eyes were vibrant and he laughed and clapped. His waning health had no discernible cause, and I had hoped Maui might perk him back up by spending time together with us, time by the sea.

Then I heard the thud.

I rushed to Davis's room where he had fallen. His head lay against the sharp edge of the floorboard corner. The rest of him lay flat on the floor. He looked perplexed.

Oh, God! What now?! Oh, God, please help him! Help me. Oh my god.

He reached for me. I struggled to help him to his feet, but I could not lift him by myself. His ability to stand was gone, and my strength to hoist him was not enough. Still, I tried, and together we slid back down to the floor leaving a bright streak of blood smeared across the wall. I could not look at the wound, not yet. I needed to help him to his bed first.

I drew in a breath to steady my thoughts.

Is this a 911 call, or do we take the trip to the ER ourselves once Rick returns from his morning run by the beach?

Davis struggled to try to stand again. I helped him scoot over toward the bed. I pulled, he crawled. Once closer to the bed, I stood up and, like a crane, I clamped my arms around his waist, and, with all the power inside me that I could muster, I lifted him. He was limp and heavy. I lifted again and again until he was back on the bed. The blood soaked into the sheets and circled his head on the pillowcase.

Okay. That's a little bit better. Hold off on 911.

As we waited for Rick, I put on a cheerful voice to calm us both down and distract us from our predicament. I had used this voice before to help a panicked friend escape a riptide and with a confused stranger on a busy highway. Shifting the tone of my voice worked to distract whoever needed distracting. This time it was both Davis and me. My whimsical tones and words reassured us, staccato style, low to soprano, as we waited.

Rick opened the door to the room and repeated my earlier mantra—"Oh my god, oh my god. What happened?" He stared at the streak of red down the wall, then came to Davis to look at the head wound.

"I heard the thud." Unspoken, I communicated that I had not been with him in the room. I felt guilty.

"ER," Rick said.

"I know," I replied.

We drove in silence to the only hospital on the island of Maui, which was forty-five minutes to an hour away, depending on traffic. I sat in the back seat with Davis in my arms. We were both bloody by now. The simple declaration of a head wound and potential shunt damage to the ER nurse by a parent in a bloody shirt gained us rapid access to help.

I hated crisis. Still, I had learned to open the door to this unwanted guest and ride the chaotic wave through to the other side of a challenging event with quiet in my heart and mind as best I could. As Davis's parent, it simply was all that I could do when I felt helpless to change a circumstance. I once stumbled upon a poem by the Sufi poet Jalal al-Din Rumi about welcoming the unexpected arrivals in our day in his poem The Guest House which helped me to do what I had always done, which is to apply meaning to what I cannot control.

The Guest House

This being human is a guest house.
Every morning a new arrival.

A joy, a depression, a meanness,
some momentary awareness comes
as an unexpected visitor.

Welcome and entertain them all!
Even if they're a crowd of sorrows,
who violently sweep your house
empty of its furniture,
still, treat each guest honorably.
He may be clearing you out
for some new delight.

The dark thought, the shame, the malice,
meet them at the door laughing and invite them in.

Be grateful for whoever comes,
because each has been sent
as a guide from beyond.

— *Jalal al-Din Rumi*

This crisis required a CAT scan of Davis's head. They did not have his previous imagery, so the film was sent to our doctors at Mammoth Hospital. They knew Davis and his history best and could better determine what action to take. We were set to travel home the next day and would go straight into the ER if they found a problem. They did.

We returned to Mammoth and took Davis to the ER the next day. By this time, he could no longer stand on his own.

The CAT scan showed a slight variation in the position of his ventricles which could be the result of the shunt.

While I was not scientifically gifted enough to recall the function of ventricles, I remembered when Davis underwent his first brain surgeries at the age of three. Then, the surgeons had to remove cysts by aspirating the cysts, or basically using a chomper I saw later on a video of the procedure to break the cysts. The remaining debris had clogged his ventricles and prevented these from draining correctly. The excess brain fluid had to be drained through an exterior and then an interior shunt. What they always tried to show me on these CAT scans when they tracked his shunt was something I could not see. But I knew that something was not working right.

The doctors decided to life-flight Davis to Reno. I went home, packed our bag, and returned to wait for the ambulance to take us to the Mammoth airport. Deena, ever the thoughtful friend, came by with a goodie bag filled with iced tea, food, and pages from a section of her upcoming book, which helped me to carry her words and life-style of positivity and gratitude along with me.

Bad weather in the Sierra Nevada mountain range prevented the plane from landing and picking us up. Plan B.

Rick and I called our entire experience with Davis "Plan B." Once, we went so far as to count every significant shift in our life plans caused by his medical condition. We arrived at the letter T. We stopped counting.

Unable to fly, we rode in an ambulance to Reno, a three-hour drive. Once in the ambulance, I remembered that I forgot to pee. As a parent dealing with years of crisis, I told myself that I had a battle-ready bladder, and mine cooperated until we got to the ER in Reno.

Davis held my hand as I sat beside his gurney in the ambulance, beside him in the emergency room hallway, and another few hours at the Reno ER in an examination room next to a noisy, obnoxious drunk who had fallen in a casino. We made it to the patient floor at two a.m., and I fell asleep on a cot beside Davis.

At seven the following morning, I held a thin blanket to my chest and stared up from my cot as the first of the physicians, a neurologist, made his rounds. Their initial tests suggested toxic levels of one of his seizure medications.

When Davis fell back asleep, I reached into my bag and pulled out Deena's manuscript pages specific to positive thinking. I was interrupted a few pages into her book. A physical therapist came in to assess Davis's balance, or lack thereof. As we walked the hallway, she held onto him by his seizure belt. He stopped too often to catch his breath, she noted—and added that his inability to move without struggling for breath could be an indication that his heart was not properly functioning.

His heart?

She pulled out an oxygen monitor to confirm her assessment. His oxygen saturation levels plummeted when he exerted himself. Like an old man, the therapist told me. But he was so young. *Was his body old?* More tests were done.

Some of the staff around us had expressions of pity, which I detested. They seemed to suggest, with their glances, that our situation was not good. After so many years of watching others watch us, I thought I would and could overlook their stares. But this never went away; in fact, the bigger the boy, the more worried the spectators appeared. I wanted them to stop in case I started to believe their perception of our life, Davis's and mine, as less than another's. I was particularly sensitive to this because of my ignorance on that beach long ago when I had watched a man behaving strangely beside his elder parents. As Davis slowly taught me over the years, my old assumption incorrect.

Were the spectators right? Did Rick, Davis, and I enjoy a less fulfilling life than others? Did Ryan and Lynnell receive a smaller dose of childhood happiness? Or did having the hard edge of sorrow help us to appreciate the softness of moments we might have overlooked? I tended to believe the latter. Leisurely mornings with a cup of coffee and a good friend or wonderful spouse and conversations that had meaning and depth came more readily because of the hard times that served as accents. In art, the shadows bring forward the main subject. Our main subject was life, well appreciated, well tucked under at the end of a day.

One technician wanted to hug me. I didn't need a hug, but I knew she did. I knew the thought behind it—*Wow, how do you do this?* But my mental reminder was always: *It's not a job. A parent doesn't quit for better pay or even for sleep.* Caretaking is something anyone could and would do if their loved ones fell sick or experienced surgery or an accident that required our attention to help them. It simply was what one did.

The heart stress test and the heart echo showed no issues. I saw the image of my son's heart beating. So powerful, so rhythmic, I placed my hand on my chest to feel the pulse of life. I let the technician hug me again. She needed it.

Amid so much new information, I turned to Deena's written words and took her advice to accept what I must, change what I could of my attitude, and feel empowered to know that I could *choose* how I approached this hard new reality of Davis's failing health. I promptly set goals for my son and myself, and I envisioned a brighter tomorrow. Positive psychology was to Deena what synchronicity was to me, a blend of which had become my hybrid belief system. I hoped that one day she would write a pocket version of these inspiring chapters specific to positivity so that I could always carry them with me.

After two days at the hospital in Reno, we returned home with the toxicity of his medication levels as the diagnosed culprit.

Once home, I turned Davis back over to the team of caretakers who helped Rick and me provide for his needs. Many were his aides from school or friends of others who had cared for Davis. His current team was great, but I noticed that they too showed signs of stress from Davis's increased needs due to his declining health. I remained close, helped when I could, and set myself up for the next few weeks on autopilot as we all waited for Davis's strength to return.

On Friday of July Fourth weekend, Rick and I were invited to our friend Doug's home for dinner with our other friends: Deena, Andrew, their daughter Piper and their running teammate, Gabe. Davis was in good hands at our home that evening, so we stepped out to enjoy time with our friends. Piper entertained us all by chasing Doug's new puppy. Rick held my hand. Unspoken between us was the feeling that *This was good!* Another Keeper Moment. A sweet interlude between recent challenging moments.

At Doug's home, I felt I was among heroes, all of them. I conjured up the hope that their positivity would rub off on me—that we were who we hang with. I had not yet popped back up to my usual self as I waited for Davis to get better. I took notice that none of them whined, ever. Well, perhaps Piper, who was five. She was entitled. But she too bounced back from a bruise so quickly that she was also an inspiration. *Note to self: stop whining.*

After we returned home, I kissed Rick and crawled into Davis's bed for the night.

"Good night, honey," Rick said to me with another hug and a kiss for the night.

"You can't pry her fingers off Davis when he is sick," Rick often told medical staff when they asked if I wanted to stay with him.

He was so right. Whether home or away, if Davis was not well, I wanted to be close if I could be. When Davis was admitted to a hospital, so was I. I had only left Davis once when a hospital down south would not allow me to stay with him. When I returned the following day, my son had slipped into a coma. I had resolved never again to let this happen.

The next morning, Davis's temperature began to climb. This had only happened a few times in his entire life, and when it did, the numbers went up fast. I had him on oxygen, and that morning he required four liters. Not a good sign. None of this was good.

"Time to go," I told Rick as I grabbed the necessary items for an ER run with a potential overnight stay. Once there, I explained to one of my favorite nurses that I hoped my monitors and thermometers were not correct.

"Pretty sure you just bought yourself a room at the inn...here, or somewhere," he replied with a gentle kindness I had grown to appreciate over the years.

I liked this nurse because he held humor present, even as he let me know what I often did not want to hear. I needed this. I smiled. When he kidded with me, when he smiled big, I believed our challenge was merely a blip and that we could all get through this latest episode of Doing Davis.

Davis's fever and lungs were as bad as I suspected. Within an hour, an X-ray confirmed pneumonia. The doctor laid out our options as a nurse poked her head in and set down a container with iced tea from Deena.

Somehow this tiny reminder of the world outside was enough to take the imaginary anvil off my chest. I could breathe easier, surrender to our upcoming overnight stay, and look forward to returning home as soon as we could. The current of this crisis would not pull me under.

Davis recovered for a few days. Then he stopped eating. Then, slowly, he began to heal again. We were used to the roller coaster of better, worse, and better again. We liked "better." His capacity to live defined my mood.

As Davis's health slowly returned, so did his voice. When I finally heard him make a loud squawk—a demand for us to address his needs—I knew he was back. That evening we were a group of three again, content once Rick came home from work. Time for dinner.

"I can make a sandwich?" I offered, as exhaustion from the recent ups and downs with Davis wafted from my body.

"Okay, sounds good," Rick replied.

"Tam or Hurkey?" I asked.

He tilted his head.

I drew in a deep breath and tried again, "Ham or turkey?"

"Ham, or Tam. Both are fine." He took the knife from my hand and led me to the couch to sit next to Davis. "I'll make them."

28

PLAN Z

"Sometimes the moments that challenge us the
most, define us.

Deena Kastor, *Spirit of the Marathon* Film

2017

Davis never did regain his balance after returning from the hospital in Reno. After a few weeks at home with no improvement, a
new CAT scan suggested it could be the shunt not working correctly
since his fall in Maui. We had addressed the toxicity of the medications, which was no longer considered the culprit for Davis's lack of
thriving. Our Mammoth doctors wanted Davis flown out to a bigger
hospital for more tests immediately. I went home, packed a bag, and
hoped it would be a days-away, not months-away, situation for us.
The ambulance arrived to take us to the airport.

In just two months, we had been to the Maui ER, back to
Mammoth, and then ambulanced up to Reno for evaluation. At
home for a few weeks of bed rest and assisted walking. Then back
to the Mammoth ER, only to now be preparing for a life-flight to
Loma Linda. Just to acknowledge the many ER moments, one upon
the other, was exhausting. I could only imagine how hard it was for
Davis. Yet, what awaited us on the other side of the crisis nagged
and worried me. We wondered what changes would occur and what
losses we would confront, if any, to Davis's capacity, his health, and
his mobility.

As the paramedics prepared Davis's gurney for the plane, the pilot introduced himself to me. I smiled in recognition. The pilot was Gary Thompson, the same pilot who had taken us to Fresno after Davis was born. Rick and Gary had sat up front, discussing the brilliant blue High Sierra lakes below as we bounced on the summer thermals, and I clutched a pillow to my C-section incision on that first trip.

I sat next to Gary on this trip as we flew to an airport near Loma Linda Hospital. The moon was rising over the mountains near San Bernardino. We landed at what used to be Norton Air Force Base, where my father had served as Chaplain before retiring. I had spent many Sundays at that base. I had ridden my horses in the hills behind the hospital as a teenager. I had driven the very same outlying roads for my driver's license test. I made a mental note to update Dad on what I saw around Norton as we left the plane in an ambulance for the hospital.

I wished that Davis could understand me if I shared these stories with him, as my parents had shared their stories of growing up with my siblings and me. I felt these were moments missed. I recognized that the sadness that crept up on me periodically was sneaking in, and I had to counter it with stronger claims for gratitude. *Davis would get top medical help at this new hospital. Davis was not in pain.* I had space in my life to surrender to our stay at Loma Linda for as long as Davis needed. Three gratitudes to cancel out a regret.

The ER at Loma Linda Hospital felt frenetic. Gurneys lined the wall, teams rushed through the hallways with patients on the gurneys, and a gurney passed by with a sheet fully covering a person, a body. Automatically, I found that I needed to be closer to Davis, as our life-flight paramedic team tracked down someone to turn us over to, records in hand for the pass. The lead paramedic, a woman, assured me that I would not be "parked." They would find me a slot in one of the rooms before they left us.

Once in a room, Davis had a preliminary assessment during which an auto accident victim was pushed in on their gurney beside us. The doctors looking at Davis hurried over to do what they could for that patient before sending him off to surgery. Then back to Davis. More patients came in, and again and again, the most critical took priority. I understood this. They moved us off to another area, finally to a small ER room with a door.

We slept. In the morning, I asked for a bathroom break, which required a nurse to stay with Davis. "Could you point me to the coffee?" I asked.

No. This was a Seventh Day Adventist hospital, and there would be no coffee or meat.

Adjustment.

Thirty-six hours later, they found a spot for Davis in a room shared with an older man in a coma. He was taken away a day or two later. I was afraid to know why. The reality of these hospital stays pulled me too close to my ultimate fear of losing Davis. I had lost both my grandmothers but missed the *transition* because they lived far away. I was terrified to watch death because I never had. My sense of this held me hostage in the aftermath of any hospital episode. What was I, if not Davis's parent? My job was to keep him alive. My heart would burst if we were not together—because children live in a parent's heart each and every moment of their existence. In recent years, I had felt rejection aimed toward Rick and me from our older children as they grew independent. This did not impact our instinct to protect, to love, and to nurture their beings and souls as best we could—though we slowly came to understand that some of our wounds were handicapping our ability to fully support Ryan and Lynnell. Unconditional love comes from those who love themselves unconditionally. Rick and I had confidence in ourselves in every facet of life except parenthood.

Oddly enough, this was when another child entered our lives: a son Rick had not known about named David. When we first learned about him, I did what any wife would do, I did the math and calculated that David was older than my relationship with Rick. I smiled as I told our older children, "We are getting a bigger circle." David was easy to love. My family and our friends embraced David. He had grown up with little and cherished so much. His gratitude always spilled over as we came to know one another. We were delighted when David fully entered our family fold by changing his last name to Wood. Gaining a new son was a tremendous gift, and the ability to check in with him and know he wanted to hear from us became a daily gift—like Davis. Both simply smiled when they were near us.

At Loma Linda, I slept beside Davis on two metal frame chairs, one serving as an ottoman so I could raise my legs. Aside from the physical discomfort, this hospital visit was emotionally trying as well. A couple of weeks before, I had read in a group email that anyone with seizures as severe as Davis's would eventually die from hitting their heads, from seizing in the wrong place (like water), or from too many seizures that cannot be stopped. I was struggling with these thoughts and seeing Davis so weak. *I am not ready for this. Can one ever be ready for this?*

On this particular weekend, Rick and I had planned to attend a workshop for an emerging group called Disability Voices United (DVU). The workshop was taking place nearby in Palm Springs. Rick was to attend even if I could not, and he drove down to check on us at Loma Linda on the way.

As he recounted:

> Four days into the Loma Linda stay, I traveled from Mammoth to see Cheryl and Davis, and hopefully, to bring both home. On the way down, I received a telephone call from Cheryl.
>
> "Can you stop by Costco for me? It is only a mile from the hospital."
>
> "Really?"
>
> In our family, I am the one who avoids the crowds at Costco. However, in this instance, I would do anything Cheryl wanted since she had spent four nights in a chair in the Neurological Intensive Care Unit wing of the hospital.
>
> "What do you need?" I cheerfully asked.
>
> "Kirkland tequila. The large bottle."

I knew then and there that she needed a break, so I purchased a bottle of Kirkland tequila and a five-pound bag of limes and snuck them into the Seventh Day Adventist hospital, past the unsuspecting security guard. Cheryl is convinced that Patrón makes Kirkland tequila. I will go with that.

It did not take long for me to conclude that this neurological ICU was a wing where people were assigned to live out their final days.

I walked in and announced, "We are outta here today!" No matter that it was not for me to decide. I set my intention. Davis would not spend his final days here.

I asked a compassionate nurse whether I could have a cup of crushed ice. Two cups, actually. She kindly accommodated my request.

We waited until the room was clear, fixed our tequilas on the rocks with limes, and toasted to health. A few hours later, the doctors released Davis. The cause of his inability to balance, his lack of vitality, was inconclusive.

Were the seizures stealing him away? His medications? His genetic condition?

Could I steal him back?

My new course of action, by now labeled "Plan Z," was to establish a team of physicians for my son. The Loma Linda neurologist had been helpful, but she transferred to a new location that did not accept our insurance. So I worked with our local doctors to set a new path for Davis in which the next time he was life-flighted, if there was a next time, we would have doctors who had at least met him before.

I needed to establish a clear path forward for Davis's treatment and finally address the fact that something could happen to Rick and me. Davis needed seamless care with caregivers and experts who could solve his odd physical malfunctions. The experience at Loma Linda and Davis's continued inability to balance shook both of us as parents.

The plan Rick and I discussed was the possibility of a rental apartment on a ground floor where his care providers would be on-site 24/7 and we could visit daily as well. We talked seriously about this plan, but then we both became busy and decided that setting this plan in motion could wait.

A year later, Davis was still weak and unable to walk some days. Paramedics had to carry him down our stairs to transport him to Mammoth Hospital for a check-up one day. Hours later, we left the hospital, still without a diagnosis. I headed home to face the difficult task of getting a weak Davis up the stairs to his bed.

For many years it had been challenging to manage Davis safely on our stairs. So many seizures had happened mid-flight that I panicked when anyone approached the stairwell with him. I walked in front, I turned away, but nothing helped. The stairs frightened me because of his history of falling on them when his legs buckled from unknown fatigue or when he seized.

When Davis and I arrived back at our home, three firefighters were waiting to carry him back up the stairs. Unbeknownst to me, the staff at the hospital contacted the EMT group to assist me in getting Davis back into his bed safely.

I cried. I loved our community. I had not asked for help, yet one call from the ER staff had summoned these men to assist Davis and me.

I decided that I could no longer rely on others to do what I could not, which was to get Davis safely up a staircase.

The next day I went to the Workforce Housing office because Rick suggested that Davis probably qualified for a low-income rental. My goal was to find a one-story living situation with easy access. Jennifer, a kind woman who ran the program, had a one-bedroom, ground floor unit for sale in a deed-restricted complex. I looked at the unit. I sucked up my maternal pride as a mom who never wanted to leave her son's side and, with Rick's blessing, started the paperwork to purchase the unit.

Plan Z contained yet one more step for Davis to have a good living situation in case Rick and I could not be there. His caretaking situation was 24/7 in our home. It would transfer over to his new place. I hated the plan for my diminished role in caretaking, yet I knew that we needed this plan for our son's sake.

It turned out to be a good plan. But before Davis could completely move in, we had five trips to make to New York City.

29

MAYBE THIS WILL WORK

"Every family cultivates a culture and lives by its
own strangeness until the strangeness turns
normal and the rest of the world looks a little off."
-Kendra Atleework Miracle Country

2018

We will never settle; we will never give up. I liked this about us, Rick and me, because when Davis picked a set of parents to surprise with his rare genetic anomaly, he chose me, the hoper and dreamer, and Rick, the goal-oriented pragmatist who believed defeat was for the others in the same game, never for him. Or in this case, for us.

We gotcha buddy. And his smile affirmed our cause.

But did we? Had we explored all our options, all the possibilities to provide our boy with a better quality of being? Did we have a bit more to unearth? Yes, we did.

We learned about a seizure clinical trial at the PMSF conference in the summer of 2016. If we opted in, Davis would receive a chemo dose targeting a specific protein that might in turn lower the number of seizures or eliminate seizures temporarily. The official description of the clinical trial was as follows:

An open-label study to investigate the safety, tolerability and efficacy of a single 6-hour intravenous infusion of AMO-01 to treat adolescents and adults with Phelan-McDermid Syndrome (PMS) and co- morbid epilepsy (ages 12-45)

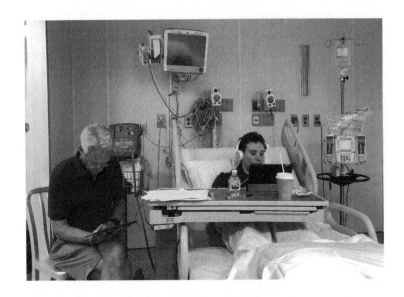

This Pilot study will examine the safety, tolerability, and efficacy of AMO-01 as a novel treatment for adolescents and adults with Phelan-McDermid Syndrome (PMS) and epilepsy. AMO-01 inhibits is an inhibitor of a pathway that is known to play an important role in neurodevelopmental disorders and seizure generation. AMO-01 will be administered once over six hours through intravenous infusion on-site at Mount Sinai. The overall study will include five visits to Mount Sinai over approximately eight weeks. Individuals may be eligible to participate if they are ages 12-45, have pathogenic deletions or mutations in their SHANK3 gene, and are diagnosed with epilepsy.

We became the first family to make the trip to New York City for the trial. We flew from Mammoth Lakes, to Los Angeles, and then on to New York City. Three flights. With a wheelchair, Davis and a service dog. We decided to combine one of the two trips and planned to remain in New York for two weeks after the drug was administered. The first two trips were a meet and greet with testing done to establish baseline capacity for Davis. How much can a person with an eighteen-month developmental baseline give a researcher? Just his smile. The staff smiled back. Not a whole lot of smart, but certainly a load of sweet in each encounter. The head of the research team told Davis he was one lucky boy to have parents as committed as he felt we were.

Rick and I talked about that in our small hotel room later. *Committed.* It was just what we always did and believed we always would do as long as we could. We knew no other path but the path of Doing Davis. To hear our roles described and complimented upon through the eyes of a clinician who worked closely with so many families tending to children who were not typical was a nice pat on the back for our efforts.

On the day the chemo drug would be administered, Rick paced about our small space, more anxious than usual. I packed up a few items for a long day and we set out on foot and wheelchair for the clinic twelve blocks away. We liked walking this city, though it was not wheelchair-friendly. We found small hubs of community on the various streets. A camaraderie in tight spaces as well as an aggressive demeaner in other locations closer to the dense crowds near Time Square. That day we were in the Mount Sinai Hospital area.

We arrived in the room, complete with a hospital bed, metal chairs and a television. It was so familiar. The staff asked if we had brought Davis's medications, just in case. We had not, so Rick walked back to the hotel room to retrieve them.

While Rick was gone, a person wearing hazmat gear brought in the IV bag of fluid. The line was hooked up, and it leaked. The valuable drug spilled onto the floor. The doctor stared at his assistant, who stared at the nurse, and all of them avoided my eyes until one of them realized that another bag was on standby, just in case. But the first bag needed to be cleaned up. It was toxic.

"We need to change rooms and start again." A hazmat team cleaned up the mess as we moved to the next location complete with bed, chairs and television. I returned to grab Davis's shoes and could not because they were contaminated and needed to be cleaned.

What had I allowed to go into my child?

Rick returned and we settled in for the long wait as the new bag was hooked up and connected to the IV in Davis's forearm. Around two o'clock I decided to head out to find food for us to eat in the room. Once on the streets I felt the panic build up. I had blocked the fear while in the room and slowly my breathing sped up and my mind grabbed onto the toxicity of the drug going into Davis. I walked around the corner, saw an Italian restaurant with a sign on the sidewalk with a welcome word: Rosé. I followed the word inside and sat down at the bar for a glass of wine and dialed Deena's number.

"You won't believe it," I began. She listened, I sipped. My breath became steady.

"Good place to be," she ended our call with. "Sip that wine."

I found a deli across the street, picked up food for us and went back into the room a bit lighter than I had been when I left. Rick and I asked to carry the IV pole down to the bathroom so that we could change Davis's diaper. The staff followed and commented on our routine. Rick steadied Davis as we removed his jeans and his two diapers. Davis sat, pooped, and was ready to be cleaned up and re-diapered. All this was done without words because it was a routine we knew so well. The staff had words, "What a team," and "You really have this down."

We really did.

Rick spent the afternoon working on client files, and on the phone with his office. As Rick chatted away, I wrote. Words on page settled my mind. Sometimes I directed the essay, but more often than not what I wrote was pulled from another well, another place, and became familiar as truth once I read the content.

By evening the chemotherapy bag was empty. We could go. The doctor suggested a restaurant or two to Rick while I helped Davis into the wheelchair. Out on the street, Rick guided us around the corner and to the same restaurant where I had earlier sipped a glass of rosé. The bartender greeted me and Rick looked perplexed.

"Uh honey," I admitted. "Remember when I went out to get lunch? And you asked if the lines had been long?"

I gave my guilty-as-charged shrug and we found a seat in a booth with Davis seated beside me. He watched his iPad while Rick and I enjoyed a glass of wine. For the rest of that trip until Davis was re-examined two weeks later, Rick and I felt more carefree exploring New York than we had on vacations elsewhere. Hampered by wheelchair and service dog, we explored museums, discovered so much about Central Park, and looked longingly at night life options we might return for on another trip when we did not have Davis with us. Part of Doing Davis meant early to bed, settled, and safe. Seizure free for those two weeks. Away from some of the stressors back home.

One of the most difficult pieces of our experience in that moment was not so much about Davis, which was and would always be a prevailing angst done to the best of our ability with a smile or a laugh when we could. But rather about the lack of connection we felt with our older two children. In particular, our daughter had left our home one day, not to return or re-engage for years without anger in her approach.

What precipitated our split will be forever examined and re-dissected with shifting perspective, but the conflict arose out of a moment of crisis with Davis.

Rick had recently spoken at a conference and met another mother who was also a speaker and had recently lost her child—to seizures. Rick emailed her to ask about her loss. He copied me on the email, which I opened only after this mother replied. Her reality was ours. She stated that eventually the seizures will claim our children. Always.

And I hated knowing what I did not want to know, unsure if there was a truth in what she was saying through her grief, and not wanting to check out that information. Period. Nope. I took my role as one to do day-by-day, not with a sense of dread but led by hope that some piece of Davis will light up a moment and show me he is content.

That same day Davis had three seizures. On his second seizure I cancelled the babysitter and my plans to join Deena's family for dinner. Rick went on to their home for a meal while Davis and I sat quietly in his bedroom. Deena texted me her one famous line, "What do you need?"

"Más tequila por favor!"

It was our joke, and she sent a shot of tequila home with Rick. I sipped the tequila and later sat with my daughter as she wanted to share with me new plans for her future. Typical scared parent, I encouraged her to consider her options fully and financially. She smelled the tequila on my breath and off we went. Both regrettably hurting.

The shadow of her absence darkened our trips to New York. We made the best we could of what we could not change just as we always had, in part surrendering, in part denying. In part retreating. Christmas during these years of her absence was not jovial or filled with family playfulness. A new formality had set in, and both Rick and I pondered whether or not this was the price to be paid for years of Doing Davis.

30

LOSING A MENTOR

"I answer the heroic question, 'Death, where is thy sting?'
with 'it is here in my heart and mind and memories.'"

Maya Angelou

2019

My dad loved hearing about the lives of his children and grand-children, the details, the plans. He read and reread my stories about Davis over the years as I wrote snippets of our experiences. He listened intently and followed up with thought-provoking questions. Ever the philosopher, he would ask, "What do you do with what you know now?"

How would I grow from a challenge met, regardless of the outcome?

It was just when Davis had 24/7 care in his own home and was successfully transitioning into his new environment in the loving hands of his care team—and my life had pivoted away from being the constant caretaker—that my father suffered a stroke on a cool autumn day at his home in San Diego. He was a few days shy of ninety-four; my mom was eighty-seven and still weak from her fall years earlier. As much as I had balanced on the precipice of life and death with Davis, I was not ready to face my parent's mortality. I never had to face the loss of someone I loved and the vacancy left in their wake. I'd been lucky in that if a part of my heart got hurt, amazing people filled the gap and reminded me that I could do more and be more—while Davis, my parents, and all of those that I loved were still in my world. On the drive down from Mammoth to San Diego to get to the hospital, I watched the sagebrush pass by, scraggly and dry. A feeling of loss and an inability to process the more difficult moments in my life pushed forward and claimed me. As a special needs parent and as a daughter of a man who had suffered a stroke, I felt defeated and unable to protect those I loved. But with Dad, I believed that I had an opportunity to try to bring him back. I decided to split my time over the next few days or weeks between Mom and Dad, just as I had after Mom's fall. Having a plan for my father's healing helped me avoid my fears on the lonely drive.

I hoped Dad was not in a wheelchair as I approached the hospital entrance. *Please be okay, Dad.*

With red eyes, I walked through the door to his hospital room. *This is bad. Emotions, please step away.*

"I hate hospitals," I reminded Dad as I made my way around to the left side of his hospital bed, away from the IV pole and the monitor. "You do too."

He gave me a semi-wink and nod that meant "Okay."

I pulled over a metal folding chair and settled in. So familiar. In every medical crisis which brought me to the hospital, each room included a sterilized bed with eighteen inches of space around it for the patient's family. Sometimes there was a chair. I still heard monitors in my sleep and reached for my son in my dreams. Every hospital room circled me back to memories of waiting for him to heal.

Dad moved his mouth, but the sound was muffled and could have been one of many words. His blue eyes diverted to the call button he could not reach with his right hand. I shifted my eyes from his fingers, frozen in my grip.

When Davis used his eyes to show me what he wanted, I immediately responded, "Good talking, buddy."

With Dad, this felt new. I refused to show concern. We needed to beat this and see what parts could heal.

"Nurse?" I asked.

He nodded.

"Pain?"

He nodded.

These affirmations were so much more than Davis could ever tell me. Dad moved his left hand towards his back. The pain was in his back. I pushed the button for the nurse and rearranged the pillows behind him. Another nod. Dad slept after receiving the pain medication through his IV line.

He looked so damn vulnerable. The awful reality was that he needed to rely on others in this situation to push a button to ask for help. He must have felt so frustrated without his independence. Davis did not know otherwise and accepted assistance for feeding and moving about his world, always in the care of others.

I struggled to make sense of losing what had been familiar as Dad's capacity. Would he heal, could he? Or would he continue to deteriorate slowly?

I was afraid. Fear was something I normally would have distracted myself from. My father's interest in my life provided me with a small sense of relevance in a world where I felt more and more invisible as Davis's dependence on me diminished. I was not ready to lose Dad as I knew him. Selfishly, I acknowledged that this was about my loss as much as his.

For Dad, if he could not speak or became trapped in a wheelchair, who would he be? Not Dad as we knew him. Not Robert as he knew himself. He had taught me so much. Rick too had such tremendous respect for my father.

Dad's eyes opened an hour later. He shifted his cheeks into the semblance of a smile. The clock on the wall clicked forward another minute. A new one. Each slower than the last. I sat on the side of his bed touching his left arm, and it was so cold. I stepped away as Dad's doctor came to his bed, but the doctor wanted me there. I knew it was bad before the doctor said what he came to say. His eyes and the somber tone of his voice gave it away. I felt the familiar gut punch even before it arrived. Our world and my place in it were about to shift.

It was time to gather the family. Dad would not rebound. Not this time. I was slow to process the meaning of this, but when I looked at Dad, he knew.

"Then I think he wants to be home, with his wife," I heard myself saying.

I remained disconnected from my tears. Time for that later. My stronger self stepped forward. I knew her well from our time together when the going got rough and it was time to paddle forward to calmer waters.

Dad nodded. The doctor asked again so that he was clear about my father's intentions. No mixed messages; Dad wanted to die near his wife and away from the hospital.

I was a caretaker and not familiar with end of days comforting. I had always focused on the survival work of keeping Davis alive. I was not sure I knew how to do otherwise. But Dad and I had talked about this for years. I knew what he wanted from his children. Could I comfort him and provide him what he needed—do what I did for Davis—but also let him go?

I made the calls to my siblings. My brothers and their wives drove over earlier in the day than they had intended. My sister would be on a plane soon from Denver.

So it began—the end.

I would be saying goodbye to a remarkable man who taught me how to meet the challenge of the unknown and Davis's rare syndrome day by day. He taught me to do just as he did during his WWII service, in which he earned a Purple Heart for his extraordinary bravery. Now he would leave my family and me with only our memories of his profound leadership and his journal notes to inspire our courage in the years ahead without him.

By the end of the day, a hospice bed had been set up in my parent's place at their care center. They had two rooms: one we had set up as a living room, the other was their bedroom. Because Mom often woke Dad up at night to assist her, we placed his bed in the living area, and Mom remained in the bedroom at night. My brother Paul, my sister Marcia, and I hired nurses to be with him around the clock. I had always slept beside Davis during a crisis, but this would require so much more of me, and I needed a place to reset each evening away from the care center. I needed that emotional evenness to assist our mother through her husband's final moments. My sister shared the room with me, and we had evenings together to talk about the past and ponder our future.

Each morning I slipped out of the room early and found a path through a fence between the motel and the care center. I would meet the night nurse to ask about how Dad was doing, and I greet the new person coming on.

My siblings and I all did our best to smooth our father's end of days transition.

Some mornings I pulled out chapters from my manuscript about Davis to tell my dad the tales he had not yet heard. I read aloud. If he were alert, he would smile. Then, about four days in, he became unresponsive.

My siblings and two of their wives felt he was passing. We sang to him his favorite songs from church and from our memories of what he sang to us when we were small. One tune had the words, "If I had the wings of an angel, over these prison walls I would fly." Not one of us had dry eyes after that tune. Dad used to sing this song in the car when we drove across the country to get to his next military assignment. This song always settled us when we squabbled in the back seat.

Our parents introduced us to so much. Hypnosis, white light healing, tarot cards, and meditation for headaches. Dad was ever the Hierophant, a scholarly and spiritual soul who disappeared into his forest of a junk shed for hours at a time. Mom was the shapeshifter, exploring all of the archetypes.

More recently, Mom had disappeared a bit more each year into dementia. As she slipped away, I lost a metaphysical partner. Dad had continued to stir his brain with books and conversations. He was well-liked at the care facility because he was always interested in others' stories rather than offering up his own. He was a listener.

The following day after our serenade, I made my way to his room full of dread. When I opened the door, I found him sitting up with his nurse brushing his hair.

"G–oo mo–n–ee," he said. I stared in disbelief.

"Good morning," I replied as I pulled out my camera. "Could you say that again? For the others? I will send it to them."

I videoed his good morning and texted it to my siblings.

The days passed like that: some good, some sad. The grandchildren began to arrive to see their grandfather one last time.

David—our new son who had found Rick and made our world bigger and happier with his personality and his smile—called me as I held vigil beside my father. He did not want me to be alone. I loved him. Always have and always will.

My sister and I also grew in our companionship during our long vigils.

I watched the grandchildren adjust to their new reality that would include life without their beloved Grampa.

These were sweet, hard, sad moments that we shared as a family.

"Oh, kiddo," my dad used to say. "You have it so hard."

"I get it, Dad," I whispered in the small hours before dawn when we were together alone before his daytime nurse would arrive. I had not understood why he continued to say this so often over the years. I did not like my situation as seen through his eyes. His blue eyes, seemingly more opaque each day as he faded. His eyes that morning met mine.

He blinked.

Here was my new challenge. One I had no choice but to accept. One I would not conquer.

How does one say goodbye?

My daughter had recently stepped away from us, from me, from her family. Another goodbye? Another tough reality. Her life felt hard, like an emotional roller coaster, and she blamed me.

I did too.

I could have and should have seen the neglect the older children felt as Rick and I Did Davis. As Dad lay dying, he too was aware of our family struggles. When we talked of this in better days before his stroke, he encouraged me to be patient. I could not coax my children to be somewhere they did not want to be. Dad had mentioned his struggles with his children. To be a parent—that rite of passage that reminds us of the thread we carry from one generation to the next—is a hard job.

"Dad," I said the next day in the wee hours when we were alone, "I am so sorry this is so hard for you. I want to make it better, and I get that we can't. And that you don't want to be here."

His face had lost its former shape, and what remained framed his cheeks. Like a skeleton.

"I am so sad for all of us, Dad."

He had not been awake or alert for days. I slept on the couch next to his bed that last night. His chest lifted mechanically with each difficult breath. His body was nearly still.

When Mom woke, I helped her with her breakfast and wheeled her into where she wanted to be, beside Dad. The brother I had always been close to, Paul, and his wife Janice came in later that morning. The room was quiet. Too quiet for Mom, whose mind, withered from dementia, did not always keep up with where she was in the world.

"What are we doing?" she asked loudly, breaking the quiet. We laughed and reminded her that we were sitting with Dad.

"I need my Vaseline," she replied. For her lips. We laughed again and tended to our mother as Dad would have.

As Dad's chest cadence changed, we said goodbye. Mom told him she loved him, and he had been a good husband. It was okay to leave;

she would be fine, she said. I leaned into his ear and began to sing the first verse of Amazing Grace. One verse, and he passed.

The broad expanse of quiet and the weight of grief collided when Dad's soul departed. One of my most wonderful mentors was gone. Even though I knew the outcome, I did not feel its impact until that moment. I still hoped for a happy ending, a miraculous recovery.

Where's our rainbow, Dad?

31

CHERYL STRAYED

"Strength doesn't come from what you can do. It comes from overcoming the things you once thought you couldn't."

unknown

2019

I pondered the beauty of death after Dad's passing, the reconciliation of our angst, our fears twirled up from our childhood memories. In this transition, would we, his children and grandchildren, hold on to what was the best in each of us and roll more stones away from our hearts? Could we manage to reflect on the stones within our hearts— baked up from memories made bolder over time—and choose to dissipate these lumps through our compassion for ourselves and one another? For me, these stones existed because I held onto the pains of my past. Resentment blocked the regenerative currents and too often funneled the energies of love and acceptance into blame. Now I chose to shift these dark shadows by exploring them through my writing and sharing my stories. I discovered that the conclusions I finally found were unique to me yet universal. Loss provided the opportunity for me to contemplate what truths served me well and what could be discarded. Marked as resolved. Roll the stone away.

But first, I grieved.

"Are you able to sleep yet?" my friend Sindee asked. Her words echoed, and before I denied them, I chose to tell the truth.

"No." I had not slept since Dad's stroke. Not without a sleeping pill, and even then, I spent a few hours struggling with my regrets, my confessions, my sense of loss in a world he used to make sense of for me. I was miserably sad and saw no way out of my despair.

After Dad's stroke, the saddest part of the "other side" was that it did not include Dad.

The pattern of darkness I felt was not new, just one more D for Depression added to the list started recently. Davis, Daughter, Dad. Davis was very much alive, healthier than he had been in three years. He lived in our town just a half-mile away from us with six alternating caretakers. My new tagline to relieve my guilt over not caretaking my adult son was that "it took six to replace Rick and me." With space in my day where he used to be 24/7, I truly grieved parts of our experience together these past twenty-four years. I had not grieved earlier because I pretended for so long that it was not as hard as it truly was. I had space to miss the man Davis could have been. I felt sad that I was not enough of a mother to manage him alone, that he needed others, not just me anymore, to keep him happy and alive. I sensed the loss of him each day, but I knew I also needed to be less tethered to his care for my health and sanity. It was frustrating not to be able to somehow, heroically, do it all on my terms. I still wanted to be with him, caring for him each day, and yet I needed to be free of the burden of full-time caring for an adult child.

I also missed my daughter, Lynnell, who had grown apart from me. The proper term was estranged. It was her choice, not ours, and one that brought us great sadness.

I had a lot of time to think during that dark winter after Dad's passing. I longed to be back outside, on a trail or in a tent. The backcountry is where hearts healed and bodies strengthened. I wanted to feel the heightened anticipation of the nearby coyote pack as they called in a full moon—with only the nylon of my tent between raw, wild nature and me, yet with my tough hiking buddy Nancy nearby who could assure me from her tent that we would be fine. I craved to hear only the sound of wildlife, water in movement, and life off the grid.

That summer, I often ventured into the wilderness with friends to heal. On one trip with some girlfriends, we were suddenly caught in a thunder and rainstorm. We scrambled to unfurl the rain flaps on each of our tents beneath the sporadic thunder. I counted aloud the seconds between the flash and the sound. The flashes came faster and faster, and then the storm moved north. We stayed up that night to deal with the water soaking our backpacks and other gear left out of the tents. On another trip, I woke up into a brilliant full moon as if the lights were on everywhere. Even the animals seemed restless with the bright beam breaking through the branches above.

My breath steadied when I imagined my feet on a trail and my mind on a destination.

I was tired of losing those I loved through lack of connection or death, through over-busy schedules, and under-mindful attention to relationships. Each chapter closed scared me as if it would be the last one in which I laughed or found contentment. Could I drag myself up from the sadness one more time? Would it make a difference if I tried?

During our December getaway to Maui, I was quieter and less available as I sorted through my sadness and my need for a new direction. As was my custom over the years each morning on that island, I set out for my morning walk. I remembered something from so long ago when I was in my twenties. A depression had sunk me, and I had returned to our family home to heal. I had decided to take a run to boost my spirits. I laced up my running shoes and left the house. In the driveway was my Dad, on a bike.

Dad did not bike. He had on his khaki pants, a tattered T-shirt meant for yard work, and a big smile. He led me forward.

"Let's do this, kiddo."

And we did: he biked alongside me as I jogged.

In Maui, running pulled me out of a funk quicker than anything. It was why I took those few precious steps each morning, not much, fifteen minutes plus a hill. Sometimes I jogged back down. On this morning, the hill wore me out. In the past, I liked the push and rewarded myself with a yip at the top. Today I was just going through the motions. I felt even more alone and empty when I recalled my memory of Dad beside me on a bike.

"You've got it so hard, kiddo," he used to say.

Until his stroke, that was what I heard and detested. I needed him to applaud my life, not to spoil my perfect portrait of Doing Davis. Denial always helped keep me a few steps ahead of sadness. I hated sadness. It frightened me, its capacity to grab and hold me down. It kept me from distracting myself with painting or quilting or chattering with friends as if all were well and right in my universe.

But he spoke the truth. He knew that I had on my mask of a smile and underneath was the stress. Dad got me. Understood me. Doing Davis was hard.

As I ran, though he had passed a month earlier, we talked just as we used to.

"It's sleep, Dad. I can't seem to sleep since you left. Your passing was hard and beautiful, all at once. I thought you would rally the way Davis always does. One more comeback still in you."

The image of Dad did not reply with words, but I understood the message.

Dad was tired. Ready. Worried about leaving his cherished wife behind because she was blind and had dementia.

I listened as my imaginary dad pedaled beside me.

He spoke of stages. His stage was to pass.

As his image remained beside me, I ran slowly. I heard him. I could do more to turn this page. The next phase would be yet another garden to cultivate and weed. Dad liked metaphors. His sermons had been my favorite. When I was a child, our chats were a bit of a puzzle until I figured out that he spoke in symbols, like myths and fairy tales, and that I had to bring home the kernel of truth on my own.

The final D had come two days earlier while we were away. We learned that our beloved dog Lucy needed to be put down. She was in pain. Her heart had a fluid buildup around it. *Please, not Lucy.* She and I had gone to service dog training every other week, seven hours away in Oceanside, so that she could be a service dog for Davis. Now she too was gone.

I had never seen Rick cry, yet when we heard the news, we held one another and cried—not just for Lucy, but for all that we had not shared our tears in response to. The years, the challenges, the life episodes that were simply part of life. All that we had been through finally struck hard. This final D knocked us over for a moment, Davis, Daughter, Dad, and Dog. I had slept most of the next day, unable to absorb an emptier life in my mind.

Now imaginary Lucy was running beside imaginary Dad, who was pedaling faster. I kept up. Lucy had her tail proudly wagging her happy wag.

I decided I was okay. Not content, but for now, *okay* would work. It was time to step into another chapter, to choose to make it as rich as the last.

My attitude was up to me, but I still wondered, *Would this new chapter include our older children? Was it their choice or ours? What could I do, or not do, to make a difference?*

Rick and I talked about our parental regrets and weighed them against what we had managed to provide for our children. The memories of our family had many sweet spots that had been overshadowed by the medical moments and our time away with Davis. Each of us would perceive our past together through our unique understanding of that history. All we could do was make space and opportunity for reconnection. I believed in rainbows on the other side of the storm.

Incredibly, just then, ahead of me in the sky that morning in Maui, a rainbow emerged. A sign, a gift.

Lucy, my brown labradoodle, and Dad, as a young army man, stood nearby smiling.

"No pain, no gain," they reminded me. In other words, pain and gain are simply part of the tough process called living.

"Yes, Sindee," I finally said when we had our next call, "I can sleep again." A combination of forces had been helping to heal me. It began with a daily reminder of all that was good around me and all that I could make better if I simply showed up with a can-do attitude for myself— just as I had for Davis for these past twenty-five years. It wasn't long before I was able to laugh, love, and share good times with good friends again.

During this time, my art shifted. My art buddy and dear friend Kimberly noted it first. Gone was the need to hold onto realism: my fiber art, my paintings, my watercolor morphed toward the abstract. This shift allowed more room for exploration and more possibility for others to find their own message in my work. Kimberly had been my art partner and mentor for so long that we knew where the other was headed artistically before grasping it ourselves. I had a special term for these friends, the special relationships I had in life with other women. I called them my "Sisters of Solution," or sos for short. We signaled and answered each other throughout our experiences together.

What I had feared for twenty-five years was whether or not I could say goodbye to anyone I loved: to Davis, to Rick, to our other children, to my parents. Whether by choice or by circumstance, transitioning in or out of relationships had been a sticky handicap in my life. My life's focus had been Davis. He was also my excuse for sometimes not showing up when others needed me. To trust my heart to another, I had to know it was also part of life to lose that person and that I would be okay. My father taught me how to say goodbye to those I love.

Epilogue

FULL CIRCLE

"Someone I loved once gave me a box full of darkness. It took me years to understand that this too, was a gift."

Mary Oliver

2021

I am often asked, "How do you do it?"

Crisis by crisis, moment by moment, pausing between the demanding challenges to savor the quiet space in between. With a pen as my walking stick and humor as my shield, I am driven by hope for a sweet spot between the storms, and hopefully not by fear of getting wet. Rick and I have learned grace and humility by taking smaller steps beside a boy who cannot walk any faster or by patiently playing beside him on the shore as he dips his toes into the foam for hours. Sometimes these settled moments come when we sit together in an emergency room, unsure of our outcome. These are all part of the great and satisfying experience of Doing Davis.

We have accepted this permanent detour toward a more meaningful journey. Garth Brooks puts it well in his song, The Dance:

And now, I'm glad I didn't know
The way it all would end
The way it all would go
Our lives are better left to chance

I could have missed the pain
But I'd of had to miss
The dance

–Garth Brooks, *The Dance*

We no longer hope or expect that the side roads will eventually link us back to the main road, the highway toward our original destination of normalcy. We have carved new hopes and dreams from the explorations and detours we've taken down so many side paths. I used to think we were lost. Then I would find a familiar face or hug a familiar soul and discover that while my feet and ego might feel anxious about our surroundings, my heart was and is always very much at home.

On a recent trip to Maui, I was walking alone on the shore of Kapalua beach when a loud noise disturbed the peace of the moment. Two men of similar size are in the water causing the commotion. One is older, greyed, and smiling. He is my husband. The other is in a life vest slapping at a ball Rick has placed in front of him. He is my son.

I kick off my flip-flops and pass a woman pointing toward my men.

"They look happy," I say and meet her gaze, "really happy."

She looks flustered, as I did years ago on this same beach when a loud, disabled man interrupted the hush of the bay, and I was caught staring.

"They're mine," I continue. "Sorry for the noise. Our boy has no words but loves to use his voice."

She stares at my men with furrowed brows. She is young, with many years to go in her life journey. *Will she have children? Will one be like my boy? Who knows.* As I pass her and our eyes meet again, I smile. She looks away as I once did.

Finally, I can appreciate the other mother's smile on this same beach decades ago. I can even imagine what the man I considered

to be strange would have been thinking as he stepped into the soft foam of shore break, as he tipped into the sea, and as he emerged to find comforting eyes to reassure him. *Yes, yes, yes.* I might have heard this had the man used words. *It doesn't hurt to fall in water. But yucky in the mouth. Oh, there she is.*

These were insights missed long ago, before Davis, when I had overlooked souls locked in a physical form that limited not who they were, but how they could or could not share themselves with me—unless I paid attention.

I like to believe that the older woman on the beach years ago was one of many souls tasked with preparing me for my journey alongside disability. My boy has grown to be a man who jumps about and expresses his delight without hesitation. Full circle, I walk in that other mother's footsteps on that same beach toward the sea, past people who stare.

I am knee high in the shore break before Davis sees me and his exclamation of joy reaches a new vocal pitch. I manage to dive in and pop up just in front of Davis. He loves this game. Rick and I take turns as the pop-up parent because we love to see him like this—joyful, free, content.

I have found my Happy Ending with people I love and who love me too.

As Davis used to be able to say before seizures and medications stole so much from his sparkle, now we are very happily...

Ah da!

2021 Letter from Rick
The Tao of Davis

The four principles of Taoism are: Simplicity, Patience, Compassion; Going with the Flow; Letting Go; and eventually, Harmony.

I am the other parent of Davis. The "Rick" in this story. I have observed and partnered in his remarkable journey. I have laughed and cried, experienced joy and sorrow over these years. As Cheryl and I move into the next phase of our lives, we can't help but reflect on our past.

I have often said that Davis's most enduring quality is courage. The will to live. What I know now is that what is beautiful and joyful must never be squandered. Davis is lucky enough to have been born at a time when medical advances have improved not just the quality of our lives, but the odds of life itself. I have been filled with admiration as I observed Davis's mother time and again do what mothers do: selflessly embracing the challenges of Davis's life while orchestrating what she knows intuitively is best for him.

I could not have known the day after Davis's birth that his journey would be different as I sat on the floor of the hospital's maternity ward, back against the wall, shoulders stooped, bewildered at the preparations being made to take Davis away that day on the first of many life-flights to come. Number 34 in the world!

Davis is an unintentional teacher. His life is one of simplicity. He lives in the moment, accepting what each day will deliver without complaint, without fear. He lives away from our home now—only one mile away though. He is cared for by six members of Team Davis. The daily uncertainty of Davis's health, his very existence, stands in stark contrast with the moments captured each day, in which his sweetness, his courage, his unadulterated expression of joy, shine through. Davis listens silently, not expressing himself with words, but with sounds. A critical question is what is he understanding, how differently he apprehends the world? When he hears words, what do they mean? We can only imagine what Davis sees in his mind when he hears us speak.

Cheryl and I observe with pride and pleasure our other children as they engage in their careers in law (Ryan), education (Lynnell), and dentistry (David). It is with gratitude that we observe the next generation coming into its own.

As for us, we continue to "give back," Cheryl by mentoring parents of children with developmental disabilities; and I by advocating for programs and services by which those with disabilities can follow their dreams and live their best lives. Davis has made his mark, has influenced so many, one person at a time. We have enthusiastically reached out to those whose journey is similar to ours to provide help along the way.

Our journey alongside Davis includes "letting go," not of hope, but of the unknown. We have found our way to harmony, punctuated by gratitude at our good fortune. In a way, the Tao of Davis is really the Tao of the Wood family.

Acknowledgements

Thank you Robert and Jean Wayne, one departed, one still here, for being extraordinary parents sharing your philosophical, magical, intuitive wisdom in guiding me forward in my life. My siblings Paul and Marcia remain a constant inspiration to me through their life choices and their compassion.

My friends are my mentors. I am blessed that we share our dreams and our commitments to one another's journey so readily. Deena Kastor, I am still not sure how such a dedicated Olympian, writer and speaker wound up laughing and crying alongside me on this journey, but this cord of friendship means so much to me. Dear Travel Tribe, Sindee Ribolli, Christine Downs and our departed vestibule of fun, Jill Boli, what we share is indescribable, and feeds me to the depths of my soul. Love you. My community companions, Lee Rodrigues, Sue Cockroft, and my women's spiritual group we dub The Durgas (Julie, Diane, Katharine, Alicia, Wendi, Elizabeth and Jarrett), you have heard this story for years and helped me so much along the way simply by listening and then offering back your sweet inspiring intuition.

Rick, my lighthouse in any storm, we continue to celebrate the abundance of friendship, family, and community we are blessed with. Your constancy, your commitment to me, to our family, and most particularly to our son Davis is perhaps the very reason this story circles back to a plateau of joy and contentment after a crisis.

Ryan and Sarah, Grace and Taylor, David, I love you so much and am made stronger and more committed to us as a family because of the challenges and the bountiful joyful experiences we have come up through together. Thank you.

Our Phelan-McDermid family, and original pioneers Rick and I became so close to, thank you. We were lost together, at first, and then together found our footing because we shared information amongst ourselves. Dr. Katy Phelan, you made this possible, you circled us up, brought us together, and gifted us with your knowledge, compassion, and commitment to the genetic anomaly you were part of discovering. Rick and I feel blessed to count you as a friend, alongside the other first families we met at the second bi-annual genetic family conference, later officially titled the Phelan-McDermid Syndrome Foundation (PMSF). Dr. Phelan is now part of the Ereriti Advisory Committee that also includes Sue Lomas and Nick Assendelft, and Dr. Curtis Rogers, who in particular provided guidance to Rick and me through our initial experiences with Davis's seizures.

A very special thank you to the two individuals who made this book possible, Joe Reidhead of Reidhead & Company and Tressa Gibbard. Your editing and your attention to detail and story line created something I am proud to share. The very process of memoire opens us up to explore what is beyond any written sentence, and you both found the nuggets of gold buried in contemplative passages.

We are each of us a piece of a beautiful complicated tapestry called life. To the many I cannot name who wove their magic into a moment or a broader experience alongside Davis, myself, and my family, thank you. Your threads enhanced the strength and pattern of the weave.

APPENDIX

PHELAN-McDERMID SYNDROME

What is Phelan-McDermid Syndrome?

Phelan-McDermid Syndrome (PMS) is a rare genetic condition associated with intellectual impairment, absent or delayed speech, neonatal hypotonia (poor muscle tone), autism or autistic-like behavior and minor dysmorphic features, most often caused by a deletion of the distal long arm of chromosome 22 or by a pathogenetic variant (mutation) in the SHANK3 gene.

What causes Phelan-McDermid Syndrome?

PMS is most often caused by a deletion of the distal long arm of chromosome 22. For this reason, PMS is sometimes called 22q13 Deletion Syndrome. The name "22q13" is refers to chromosome "22", the long arm which is called "q", the region affected is "1" and the band is "3". The deletion can result from various types of structural changes.

The most common structural abnormality in PMS is a simple deletion in which there is one break in chromosome 22 that causes the distal segment to be lost. An interstitial deletion occurs when there are two breaks in the long arm and the intervening segment is lost. A ring chromosome occur when there are two breaks—one on the distal short arm and one on the distal long arm—so the ends of the chromosome are lost but the new end join to form a circular chromosome (ring). Most deletion of 22q13 are de novo, or sporadic, events and are not inherited from a parent. Deletion sizes can vary from less than 1 kilobase (kb) to greater than 9 Megabases (Mb).2

An unbalanced translocation results 22q13 is deleted and replaced by a segment from a different chromosome. Sometime a parent may carry a balanced translocation. As in the figure below, in a balanced translocation, a segment from the blue chromosome has traded places with a segment from the yellow chromosome. The individual who carries the balanced translocation carries the correct amount of genetic information but in a different arrangement that usual. This individual is referred to as a translocation carrier. When this carrier has offspring, they are at risk of passing on only one of the rearranged chromosomes. If the yellow/blue chromosome is a rearranged 22, then this offspring would be deleted for the distal segment of 22q but have an extra copy of the segment from the blue chromosome. In about half of the case of unbalanced translocations, one of the parents is found to be the carrier of a balanced translocation. This means there is risk for future pregnancies to have an unbalanced chromosome constitution. In the remaining cases, the unbalanced translocation was a sporadic event with no increased risk to future pregnancies. Other less common structural changes may also result in deletion of 22q13 and lead to PMS.

Pathogenic variants of the SHANK3 gene can also lead to PMS. The SHANK3 gene is located on the distal long arm of chromosome 22 and codes for the SHANK3 protein which is present in many body tissues but especially abundant in the brain. In the brain, the SHANK3 serves many functions including supporting the integrity of the synapses between neurons and in the maturation of dendritic spines. Pathogenic variants can cause complete loss or partial loss of SHANK3 and results in autism or other neurobehavioral issues.

What are the features of Phelan-McDermid syndrome?

The earliest presenting sign of PMS is often neonatal hypotonia. This means that the infant has poor, or floppy, muscle tone. This weak muscle tone can continue into early childhood, so that the typical milestones of sitting, rolling over, crawling, and walking are delayed. With time, the child may demonstrate mild to severe intellectual impairment, delayed or absent speech, and autism or autistic-like behavior. Sleep disorder, seizures, and gastroesophageal reflux are other problems that are of concern to parents.

Individuals with PMS have a decreased perception of pain. This means they do not respond as you would expect a typical child to respond to a headache, ear infection, or broken bone. Parents and caregivers must be extremely vigilant to detect any difference in a child's behavior that may indicate that they are in pain. Individuals with PMS usually have decreased perspiration which puts them at risk of overheating. They must be carefully monitored so they do not get dehydrated when in high temperature environments.

Facial features that are observed in greater than 50% of individuals with PMS include long eyelashes, full or puffy cheeks, deep-set eyes, puffiness around the eyes, wide nasal bridge, large ears. and a bulbous nose. Infants and young children often have thin, poorly formed toenails that peel off easily. As the child ages, the toenails may get thicker and become ingrown. During the teenage years, some individuals develop lymphedema of the lower extremities.

The diagnosis of PMS should be considered in infants with hypotonia, individuals with intellectual disability with or without autism and/or atypical physical features, and in individuals with lack of speech with or without atypical physical features.

How similar are individuals with PMS?

Deletion sizes, SHANK3 mutations and the features of Phelan-McDermid Syndrome are all highly variable. Because the deletion size is so variable, the range and severity of features is also variable. There is a tendency for individuals who have a large deletion of 22q13 to have more serious feature than individuals with small deletions of 22q13. This seems to be a trend but there is not a 100%

correlation between deletion size and severity of features. Genes on other chromosomes contribute to an individual's physical and intellectual development and, in the case of PMS, recessive gene on the non-deleted chromosome 22 may now be expressed that would not be expressed if both copies of chromosome 22 were intact.

How is PMS treated?

Treatments for PMS are targeted to the symptoms. For example, if an individual has epilepsy, the physician must find the best therapy for that individual's seizures. If an individual has behavior issues, the therapies will focus on managing the behavior in that individual. There is no one treatment that works for all individuals with PMS although several clinical trials have been performed and are continuing to attempt to find medications to ameliorate symptoms of PMS.

It is important that therapies begin in early childhood to address muscle tone, communication, behavior, and intellectual development. Physical therapy, speech therapy, communication therapy, sleep therapy, and others should be considered if appropriate.

How Phelan-McDermid syndrome rare?

As of December 2020, the Phelan-McDermid Syndrome Foundation's (PMSF) membership and patient registry include over 2600 individuals who have been diagnosed with PMS. However, we know that PMS is underdiagnosed. This is often because the individual was diagnosed at an early age with autism or cerebral palsy and has not had a genetic test for PMS. Another way an individual may go undiagnosed is if they had a genetic test that was not sensitive enough to detects PMS. For example, an individual may have had a test to detect a very small deletion of chromosome 22 it would not detect a pathogenic variant of SHANK3.

It has been estimated that SHANK3 deletions or pathogenic variants occur in about 0.5% of individuals ascertained for autism spectrum disorders and 0.3% of individuals with intellectual disability.

How is PMS diagnosed?

There are two common tests for Phelan-McDermid syndrome. One is a chromosomal microarray (CMA) and the other is next generation sequencing (NGS). The CMA will find loss or gain of chromosomal material, so it is ideal for finding deletions of 22q13. If gain of material from a second chromosome is also detected, the results may infer an unbalanced translocation. This will often mean a follow-up FISH test to confirm that an unbalanced translocation is present and, if so, will lead to parental chromosome testing. The CMA can tell a deletion of 22 is present but cannot identify if it is a simple deletion or a ring chromosome. For this reason, a chromosome analysis (karyotype) is recommended as a follow-up when a deletion is detected by CMA. This is because ring 22 is associated with an increased risk of developing the genetic condition neurofibromatosis type 2 (NF2). NF2 causes tumors (usually benign) to grow alone the nerves and can lead to hearing loss, tinnitus, balance problems, and headaches. The gene for NF2 is located at 22q12.2 so it is present on the normal 22 and the ring 22. The problem arises because ring chromosomes are unstable during cell division and may be lost resulting in a daughter cell with only one copy of chromosome 22. If a pathogenic variant in the NF2 gene occurs on the remaining copy of chromosome 22, the individual can develop NF2.

NGS is performed to detect pathogenic variants in the SHANK3 gene. This method examines the DNA sequence to identify if an error or "misspelling" is present that would lead to partial or complete loss of function of SHANK3. In addition to PMS, pathogenic variants of SHANK3 have been identified in Alzheimer disease, bipolar disorder, autism spectrum disorder, and schizophrenia.

The Phelan-McDermid Syndrome International Registry (PMSIR) has the largest database of diagnosed cases of PMS in the world.

THE AUTHOR

Cheryl Wood is the parent of a child with a rare genetic condition called the Phelan-McDermid Syndrome (PMS) that limits her son's intellectual and physical development and presents an array of medical challenges. Her blogs about the world of special needs can be found at www.CherylJWood.com along with photos of her son Davis. She served as the first state coordinator for the Phelan-McDermid Syndrome Foundation regional family support group and co-led conference presentations on various PMS topics such as seizures, relationships, and caretaking. She began journaling their family journey when her son was two years old. Over the years she has been part of various women's journaling groups and has mentored others on the healing aspects of tracking one's life story through pen and page.

She received a MBA from University of California Irvine and is currently a resort real estate broker in the High Sierra. Cheryl served as Chairperson for Measure C sponsored by The Mammoth Lakes Foundation (MLF) where she served on the board. The bond measure had been a vision of Mammoth Mountain founder Dave McCoy. Measure C successfully brought the first community college buildings to the Eastern Sierra. The college campus has continued to grow over the years serving both local students and students from out of the area who wish to be part of the mountain experience.

Made in the USA
Columbia, SC
01 March 2022

56763901R00143